# babycook book

David Rathgeber
and
Laurence Bonnet

# Preface

## Nothing but happiness!

I am a cook. I am writing this book for my son Alphonse, his mommy Mi, her friends, and for other young mothers who have the same desire and concern: giving their children the best market-fresh fruits, vegetables and ingredients, while at the same time introducing them to new tastes and smells from here or elsewhere. Mi is Swedish, but at our table, her childhood dishes go perfectly with recipes from various regions of France.

It was Mi who bought our Babycook when Alphonse was born (he is now two years old), to prepare the follow-up formula with fresh ingredients that keep most of their vitamins, minerals, and trace elements because they are steamed. But, as time went on, and especially with the rich variety of colors and smells available at the market, she wanted to move away from the more classic purées and compotes, and share with her son the pleasure of preparing (together) and tasting (her, too) "Alphonse's special dishes," which are quick and easy enough to prepare that they can be enjoyed every day. OK, but which ingredient should I choose and why? How should I cook it so that it brings happiness every time it's prepared?

I created these recipes in the same way that I devise my restaurant's menu: by season, with good ingredients from the market. Each flavor highlights the flavor of one product, sometimes seasoned with an herb, seasoning, or spice, or enhanced with a special pairing.

When a vegetable is the main ingredient of a recipe (I love vegetables!), I follow in Alain Ducasse's foot steps by playing with the "raw and cooked" and "crunchy and tender" nature of vegetables, to help children discover vegetables in many different forms as often as possible. I use playful presentation to help pique the child's curiosity and tempt him to nibble the bits on his plate or dip his finger in.

Of course, these discoveries must be made progressively. I designed Babycook Book recipes that will evolve as baby does, while respecting the rules of nutrition and giving directions that moms can adapt to their child's development, following each child's own rhythm, and the advice of his or her pediatrician.

The tastes presented in these recipes will become richer and more refined as baby grows and develops. With time, you will be able to feed baby more precious ingredients: a green onion added to the vegetables in the steamer basket; young, raw spinach leaves added to the blender bowl to bring out a brighter color in a dish; a thin drizzle of olive oil; freshly chopped parsley to garnish a dish; or a few grains of fleur de sel to add taste.

The consistency of dishes will be modified when blending, depending on the number and length of the pulses, and the firmness of the product. The technique will not be the same for a cherry as it will be for a fava bean! It will also depend on the quantity of sauce, water, milk, or crème fraîche added to the ingredients between pulses. We will start with a velouté or soup that is thin enough to be drunk from a bottle. Then, we'll move on to a thin purée for babies just starting to eat with a spoon. Next, when baby starts to chew, we'll serve a purée with the consistency of "caviar," and finally to end up with purées with small pieces that baby will eat when some teeth have grown in.

I have organized the Babycook Book's 77 recipes according to the logic of a mother's day: by family of ingredients. Naturally, vegetables make up the lion's share, which should satisfy pediatricians and nutritionists because vegetables are often neglected despite their nutritional value.

Each recipe indicates the recommended minimum age (to be followed prudently as a rough guide) and season(s), so that the ingredients will be at their peak in terms of quality.

The first chapter is a preview of the rest. It is dedicated to first experiences: the approach and mastery of the Babycook appliance; teaching mom about cooking baby's "meals"; and baby's likes and dislikes. At 6 months, Alphonse was already clearly expressing his satisfaction at or his disapproval of a new taste, before later (almost always) enjoying it. At 18 months, he liked beets, certain types of cheeses, dill, and pickles.

All of the recipes in the Babycook Book are presented with their good points (according to cooks and nutritionists), and with my advice as "Chef Dad" for choosing ingredients and possible ways of modifying the recipe.

Now it's time for moms to take over and put their imaginations to work, because culinary diversity and food diversification go very well together...

**David Rathgeber**
Chef at "Aux Lyonnais"
Babycook Book's Chef Dad

# Contents

# So many discoveries to be made in the kitchen with mom...

6

**Here we are. The little guy is 4 months old. He is about to start his exploration of the big, wide world by starting with the most essential part: how life tastes. And life, for the time being, with the exception of mom's arms and Dad's tickles, consists of the contents of his bottle. Cereals, simple compotes, and soups will give him a first taste, and prepare him for the transition from heart-to-heart to face-to-face, for the tender dialogue that baby's meals will become.**

**As a newborn, he knew how to breast-feed. He could recognize sweet, salty, acidic, and bitter tastes.** Now it's time for him to refine those sensations and give his opinion of these discoveries with the facial expressions at his disposal. If he doesn't like something? Don't force him. You can have him taste it a few days later, and then again... And if he still doesn't like it? Then that just means he has a personality and his tastes are asserting themselves!

**Now he's a little bit bigger. He feels his bottle, and picks up and sucks on everything he can get his hands on.** At around 5 months, he learns to open his little beak for a spoon, without pushing it away with his tongue. And at around 6 months, can drink from "his" cup. Soon he will smile his first toothy grin. And at around 7-8 months, he'll transition from his bouncy chair to a highchair to be in a better position when mom, with her Babycook at her side, rings the dinner bell...

**...and no one likes to wait when his tummy is rumbling!**

**Now it's time to introduce a new "salty" snack** (which actually should not be salty at all, or barely, before the age of one, and only slightly even then!) **or a different texture,** because, after all, baby is eating less puréed foods than before and will soon, with the arrival of molars, be able to eat mini-bites of whole food, between 12 and 18 months.

**Mom, who knows what we like, has set the highchair with baby's colorful dishes, decorated with designs** that he will discover with delight little by little after each bite of this newfound flavor. Isn't that what mom had him taste a tiny spoonful of last week, to see if he liked it? Or to see if he might have an allergic reaction? Or maybe for both reasons.

**Sometimes, she makes a pretty design with the purée. He puts his fingers in it** (she always washes them before dinner time) and picks out little pieces. She laughs and says, "Don't worry, you're wearing your long sleeved bib." She tells stories about what is on his plate. He answers her and she pretends to understand. That's how the conversation goes.

**Don't bother bringing toys to the table. They'll only distract him,** and what a pity that would be! Anyway, the food on his plate is quickly finished, without mom even having to insist, because she has perfectly calculated the portions. And if he's still hungry, she's sure to be able to find a piece of cheese.

**The best time is market time, almost every day, "so we only eat the freshest produce,"** says mom. Wide-eyed, we look at all the piles of colors, breathe in the smells, taste the samples that the merchants give to mom and baby (and Dad, too, on Sundays) when she asks for their advice. Because mom only wants "young, seasonal vegetables," "ripe fruit," "farm-fresh eggs," "fish right out of the water" (she asks the fishmonger to "bone it"), and "tender meat" that she has the butcher grind right before her eyes.

**No time for dilly-dallying! Mom wants to put our purchases away quickly, so as to "not to break the cold chain." Mom puts the frozen foods right into the freezer, right next to the little dishes that she freezes for baby** (in individual portions) when she cooks them beforehand because he really likes them or because the vegetable is really big (like a pumpkin, for example!) and the whole family can enjoy it.

**She wraps everything with plastic wrap before placing it in the refrigerator so that "the smells don't mix together."**

**And finally, she places the fruit, melons, etc., in separate baskets on the table, making sure they don't touch.** Mom knows that fruit containing water should never be put in the refrigerator, so as not to "ruin" their smell. Anyway, they won't have time to bruise because we will have eaten them by the day after tomorrow.

**But it's when mom is preparing baby's dinner (at the last moment) that we are the most attentive.** She gets our "her" Babycook appliance and "her" Babycook Book (those two are always hanging out together).

**And our mouths start watering...**

# With new foods come new flavors. But at what age?

8

**Food diversification is in some ways a treasure hunt, a quest that all children experience. During this quest, they take advantage of their evolving abilities and explore the world - stealthily - for tastes and flavors. Don't worry about their caution; there are reasons for it. Curiosity will win them over in due course, if it is encouraged.**

**He is 4 months old. Breast milk and formula no longer provide enough energy to fuel his growth spurts.** At 3 years old, his birth weight will be tripled, his sized doubled, and his brain will already have accomplished the majority of its development.

**And yet his digestive system is still in the process of developing and will be for a bit longer.** As time goes on, his stomach will be able to digest certain proteins (we choose them). His liver will reach maturity around the age of 3. Until then, he will only be able to digest fat in small amounts (we avoid them). His pancreas only produces a very small amount of insulin until the age of 6 months and then only slightly more until the age of 3, which barely stimulates the assimilation of sugars (we forget them for as long as possible), except for starch. His kidneys only start eliminating salt at 3 months (he barely needs any before the age of 1). His intestines are sensitive to everything except soft fibers (keep things soft!). And he will not have an immune barrier for several months after birth, so we stay away from foods that cause intolerances (gluten) and allergies (iodine, egg yolk, strawberries, etc.).

**Each food has its good and bad qualities,** except for breast milk, "nature's wonder food." Nevertheless, this food must be complemented and eventually replaced.

**But no one food contains all of the nutrients necessary for a balanced diet** of a quickly growing baby. And yet the body cannot produce all of the essential vitamins, minerals and trace elements that it needs every day.

**So? A varied diet will be the best way to guarantee a healthy and fit body, as well as a good way to ensure happy taste buds,** so long as parents start early and take the opportunity when baby is fascinated with discovering new things, because each new food is another addition to the range of familiar colors, smells and flavors. If parents wait too long, baby will become suspicious of the unknown and it will be too late to convince him to try everything. Take it slowly, though. Dinnertime must be a special time of the day. Shhhh! We are tasting!

**When it comes to food diversification, each baby follows his or her own nose. The pediatricians' advice is there to guide moms.** The contents of baby's bottle shows moms how big their baby's stomach is growing. And baby's reaction to food, his size-weight ratio, and his appetite for life show moms if baby is eating right. But the road ahead is still a guessing game.

**But there is a common road map.**

**Basic until the age of 3: milk, always and forever, for its unique richness in animal proteins and calcium.** If baby already has deficiencies in iron, calcium, etc., he is not eating a diverse enough diet. Absolute minimum: 1/2 liter per day after 6 months, including dairy products. But no cow's milk before 1 year old and then only in dairy product or cheese form until the age of 3. Milk is not easily digestible and is not rich enough in two very precious elements: iron (to oxygenate the red blood cells) and essential fatty acids (that help the brain to develop). So? Prepared baby formula from 4 to 12 months, and milk-based pediatric nutritional supplement from 1 to 3 years old. And that's it. And if possible, assorted "just for baby" dairy products.

**Nutritious: grains, starting at 4 months old,** for their carbohydrates (such as starch), in addition to milk sugars, and for their calories, wheat, barley, and oats, as well as rice and corn (gluten-free). In the bottle first, and in pasta, desserts or snacks later on.

**Remineralizing and revitalizing: fresh fruits and vegetables, with soft fibers, starting at 4 months old.** Cooked – no raw veggies before 1 year old. And in growing quantities that become fancier over time. For their vitamins, mineral salts, and trace elements, and for their water content, both thirst quenching and hydrating in summer.

**The almost perfect egg, starting at 5-6 months.** Starting with the yolk (hard), which, if it contained carbohydrates, would be the perfect food. Wait till 8 months to give baby the white.

**Full of vitamins: butter, starting at 4-6 months,** raw, in small amounts (vitamins A and D). A little crème fraîche, the lightest of the fats, given to baby on the end of a teaspoon. Small drizzles of olive oil starting at 6 months (vitamin E and essential fatty acids).

**Rich in protein: poultry, perfectly lean; boiled ham (without fat); and red or white meat, but lean! Starting at 6 months.** Essential for the quality of their protein and iron, and easier for the body to assimilate. But in small portions until 3 years old (portions are usually 3 times too large!).

**Full of iodine, fluoride, phosphorus, and selenium: unlimited amounts of lean fish, starting at 6 months.** To grow big and strong, with teeth for taking a bite out of life. The only fatty fish recommended is salmon, for its essential fatty acids and vitamin D, a vitamin that is crucial for the body's assimilation of calcium and phosphorus.

**For everything else, we wait:** 15 months for fava beans and omelets; 18 months for cabbage, lentils, chickpeas, and chocolate; at least 2 years for shrimp and shellfish; 3 years for figs and nuts; and 7 years for whole-grain bread.

**No need to rush. It's better to thoroughly explore the palette of flavors already at baby's disposal!**

# Chef Dad's Market

**Almonds:** Powdered at 3 years old. Whole at 4 years old, but not before so as to avoid swallowing down the "wrong tube," even if they are rich in fat, protein, minerals (calcium, magnesium, etc.), trace elements (manganese), vitamins (E and B9), and fiber. **114-115**

**Apple:** Valuable from 4 months because they are rich in water, sugar, vitamin C (the Reinette reigns over this category), balanced micronutrients, and soft fiber (pectin). Choose ones that are firm and shiny (but not waxed). If eaten raw, cut immediately before serving, or sprinkle the pieces with lemon juice so that they do not turn brown. **48-49, 105**

**Apricot:** A golden-colored fruit (carotenes) with sweet flesh (carbohydrates) and soft fibers (facilitating passage through the intestines). Rich in potassium. Baby can start enjoying this fruit at 5-6 months old. Apricots do not ripen after picking. **122**

**Artichoke:** Full of minerals (potassium, calcium) and carotenes. Artichokes contain inulin, which helps the body to assimilate minerals and keeps the intestinal flora in balance. Babies under 6 months should not eat them because of their high fiber content. **28-29, 46-47**

**Asparagus:** This natural diuretic is tender and loaded with vitamins (C, B9, carotenes) and minerals. Grown in the great outdoors, green asparagus has more taste than its white relative. It can be found in markets from mid-February to the end of June. Store it raw in a bunch for up to 4 days in the refrigerator, wrapped in a damp cloth or newspaper, with the points up. **36-37, 46-47**

**Avocado:** Imported from Israel, Florida, and South America all year round. Buy medium ripe, or when it gives a little when lightly touched (without pressing too hard, to avoid bruising). Let ripen at room temperature for a few days. The only fatty fruit, it's high in potassium, and especially essential fatty acids and vitamin E. Not to be eaten before 1 year old because a child's digestive system cannot assimilate it before then. Prepare it immediately before serving. Sprinkle with lemon juice so the flesh won't turn brown. **44-45**

**Balsamic Vinegar:** Grape must-based, aged in barrels (balsamic vinegar from Modena is aged for more than 20 years). Slightly acidic, with a sweet taste. **52-53**

**Banana:** As sweet (and nourishing) as it is yellow and spotted. Let ripen at room temperature because this tropical fruit does not like the cold! This fruit is full of potassium, magnesium, vitamin B, starch, and soft fibers. Baby's intestines can handle it at 4 months. **21, 122**

**Basil:** Herb with tender branches and sweet leaves. Always used fresh. The base for pesto. **27, 40-41, 43, 44, 62-63, 90-91**

**Bay Leaf:** An aromatic leaf often used in small quantities along with thyme. Remove from dish before serving **26**

**Beef:** Steak from 5-6 months. Rich in protein, iron, zinc, and vitamins B1 and B2. Have the butcher grind it in front of you, and then serve it to your child within 3 hours. Or buy it frozen with at least 5% fat **82-83, 84-85**

**Beets:** Well-liked when cooked because they are very sweet (sucrose), beets can also be enjoyed raw from 1 year old. **84-85**

**Blackberry:** For its vitamin C and sugar content, plus its balance of minerals, trace elements, and vitamins. Starting at 6 months. **116, 122-123**

**Blackcurrant:** Competes with the kiwi for vitamin C and calcium content. Good for baby starting from 4 months. **122-123**

**Blueberry:** Great for vision ("the fruit of airplane pilots") and the digestive system. Good for babies over 6 months. A summer berry that can be bought frozen in winter for its high levels of vitamin C. **116**

**Boiled Ham:** As rich in protein, iron, potassium, and calories as red meat. For babies over 5-6 months, as long as it is boiled, lean (or extra lean), and of high quality (off the bone, for example). **26, 62-63, 72-73**

**Broccoli:** The number 1 vegetable in vitamin C and calcium. Recommended from 4 months on. Choose one at the market with small, tightly closed buds between May and November. Light, easily digestible, and with soft fibers, broccoli goes well with salmon (starting at age 1) and other soft-fleshed fish. **34, 70-71, 92-93**

**Button Mushrooms:** Very rich in mineral salts (potassium!), trace elements, and vitamins B, D and K. Choose young, white mushrooms with no dark spots. Good for babies over 1 year old. **87, 94-95**

**Cabbage:** Can be found at the market all year round. Rich in vitamin C. Not to be given to baby before at least 18 months because its high fiber and sulfur content make it hard for little stomachs to digest. **39, 74-75**

**Cabécou:** Semi-fresh goat cheese. **27**

**Capers:** A tonic and diuretic. **100-101**

**Carrot:** When cooked, this vegetable is good for baby starting at 4 months if it is organic or from your garden (to avoid too many nitrates in the cooking water). Not to be served raw (grated) until baby is 1 year old. Buy "new carrots" from the end of April till the end of July, and "in season" carrots until mid-December. New carrots should be crispy and colorful, with fresh greens on top, and can be kept for several days in the refrigerator without losing their carotene content. They contain fiber that helps intestinal transit. **22, 32-33, 46-47, 50-51, 56-57, 80-81, 84**

**Cauliflower:** Tender, with a good dose of micronutrients and fiber (cellulose). Good for 1 year olds and older **39**

**Celery:** Both celery root and celery stalks are rich in cellulose. Can be eaten at 8-10 months **40-41, 50-51, 56-57, 80-81**

**Cherry:** Full of fructose, vitamin C, minerals, trace elements and soft fibers. This fruit is one of the first alternatives to milk lactose that can be given to baby, starting at 4 months (but always pitted until 4 years old!). It is fragile and bruises easily at room temperature, but contains too much water to be kept in the refrigerator. Choose firm, colorful, not overripe cherries with green stems and shiny skin. Eat them within 48 hours of picking. **106-107**

**Chervil:** Carotenes, vitamins C and K, calcium and potassium. Baby can eat this fairly young. **24-25, 68-85**

**Chestnut:** Fruit of the chestnut tree. Rich in fat. **48-49,116**

**Chicken** (breast): Skinless! Light and easily digestible starting at 5-6 months. Lean and full of protein, with a good amount of iron, potassium, phosphorus, and B vitamins. **70-71, 80-81**

**Chickpeas:** Nutritious and calorie-filled. Packed with vitamins, minerals, and trace elements. But they should not be given to babies under 18 months because of the fiber and sulfur content. An ingredient in hummus, falafel and couscous. Choose them white, without wrinkles. Soak them overnight before cooking. **58-59**

**Chives:** Herb loaded with vitamin C, calcium,

and magnesium. To be tried at around 1 year old. **68, 100-101**

**Chocolate:** Toning (iron), energizing (calories), strengthens the immune system and nerve equilibrium (magnesium, potassium). Starting at 18 months. **120**

**Cinnamon:** Sweet spice for babies over the age of 1. A stimulant and antiseptic that helps when baby's tummy hurts. **69, 121**

**Cloves:** Stimulates the appetite. Contain eugenol, an antiseptic used for stomach problems and toothaches. **121**

**Cod:** The leanest fish and one of the richest in potassium. Thin and firm, its flesh separates into "petals" after cooking. Good for baby at 5-6 months. **92-93**

**Coriander:** Lemony spice, in seed or powder form. **26, 44, 78-79, 80-81**

**Cornichons (pickles):** Add taste. Not to be used in excess (because of the acidity). **100-101**

**Couscous Semolina:** Carbohydrates and protein. After 6 months (because of possible gluten allergies). When cooked, it absorbs 3 times its weight in water **82-83**

**Cucumber:** A cousin of zucchini, gherkins, and melons. A thirst-quencher and diuretic because it is rich in water. A good source of vitamins and minerals (including all the B vitamins). Choose small ones that are dark green, with a smooth, tight skin, because there will be less seeds and the fiber will be easier for baby to digest (after 8 months). **40-41**

**Cumin:** A spice with a warm, distinctive aroma. **78-79**

**Curd Cheese:** A modern-day version of curdled milk. Rich in protein, phosphorus, magnesium, vitamins A, B and D, amino acids, and of course, calcium! For babies over the age of 1. **68**

**Curry:** A blend of Indian spices **39**

**Dill:** Plant with a hollow stem. A stimulant, antiseptic, diuretic and anti-inflammatory. **92-93**

**Dry-Cured Ham:** Also simply to add flavor to a "grown-up" dish. **56-57**

**Eggplant:** This cousin of the tomato contains potassium, carotenes, and fiber. Choose one with smooth, tight, and very shiny skin, a uniform color and a fresh, green stem. Can be eaten starting at 1 year old. **43, 62-63**

**Endive:** Easily digestible both raw and cooked. Soft fibers. Good for babies over 1 year. Rich in water, minerals (potassium, calcium), trace elements (selenium), and vitamin B9. **52-53**

**Fava Bean:** Rich in protein, fat, and fiber, and loaded with iron and copper (which the liver uses to incorporate iron into the blood). Buy them when they are young and tender in the spring. Peel the skin under the pod off so that they will be tender and easily digestible after cooking. For babies over 15 months. **32-33, 46-47, 54-55**

**Fennel, or sweet dill:** A medicinal plant since ancient times, this Mediterranean anis-flavored leaf vegetable is one of the richest fresh vegetables in water and sodium, and has a good amount of vitamins (A, B9, and especially C). **46-47, 90-91**

**Fig:** Rich in calcium and fiber (pectin). Choose soft figs with firm stems. For children over 3. **123**

**Flat-Leaf Parsley:** Extremely good for your health! Flavor baby's soup and purées with parsley juice and, later on, with finely chopped leaves. This way baby will be able to enjoy the herb fresh, with its richness intact (potassium, calcium, magnesium, vitamins C and K, and carotenes). **26, 38, 46-47, 52-53, 62-63, 86-87**

**Fromage Blanc:** The dairy product that is richest in protein. Gives yogurt a run for its money

in terms of calcium and calories. For babies over the age of 1. **64-65, 69**

**Garlic:** Rich in nutritional value. An antioxidant and a germ and allergy fighter. New garlic, without its germ, is easily digestible. **27, 40-41, 54-55, 62-63, 94-95**

**Ginger:** This root is loaded with good qualities. It aids digestion, improves vision, and relieves breathing problems. And as an infusion, it fights coughs, the flu, and nausea. **121**

**Grapes:** The sweetest fresh fruit. Full of minerals (potassium) and rich in fiber. Give seedless, skinless grapes to baby from 4 months. With seeds from 4 years. **48-49**

**Grapeseed Oil:** **56-57, 86-87, 116, 118-119**

**Green Beans:** Light and easily digestible. Full of minerals (calcium) and vitamins (B9, carotenes). Rich in fiber. For babies over 4 months. Choose very thin beans. **35, 50-51, 80-81**

**Hen's Eggs:** By them "farm fresh," "organic," or "free range." The yolk is good for babies over 5-6 months (serve carefully to test for possible allergies), whereas whites should not be served before 8 months (both of them always hard-cooked). Soft-boiled eggs at 1 year, fried eggs and omelets starting at 15 months. The yolk is better for baby because it is extremely rich in phosphorus, calcium, iron, iodine, and vitamins A, D, E, and B9. And let's not forget protein, fat and calories. iodine, and vitamins A, D, E, and B9. **23, 62-63, 64-65, 82-83, 86-87, 98-99, 116, 118-119, 121**

**Honey:** Contains sugar, of course, but also a good dose of iron, vitamins and micronutrients. Make sure to buy a pot with the name of the floral source and/or the region where it was produced. Acacia honey, which is clear and thin, is the sweetest variety. **69, 122-123**

**Kiwi:** Starting at 6 months old. You know this fruit is loaded with vitamin C, but don't forget about calcium and iron, too! You can buy them firm and then ripen them next to an apple (farmer's tip). **110, 122**

**Lamb:** A tender meat (protein, vitamin B, phosphorus, and especially iron!). Baby can enjoy it at 5-6 months old. **78-79, 80-81**

**Leek:** A winter staple. But spring leeks, which are fragrant and delicate, are better for children (from 4 months). To be eaten often for its minerals, fiber, carbohydrates, vitamins, and diuretic effect. Choose them very fresh, long, straight, and white. The green tops should be straight and very green, even if we only give the white part to baby. Can be kept raw in the refrigerator for several days. Does not keep well cooked. **38, 70-71**

**Lemon:** Vitamin C and calcium. Use lemon juice to keep avocados, mushrooms and apples from turning brown. **28-29, 44, 48-49, 52-53, 90-91, 92-93, 96-97, 104, 106-107**

**Lentils:** Has important qualities. Rich in protein, carbohydrates and vitamins; high in iron, just like spinach; a lot of easily digestible fiber (but very little cellulose), which makes them good for babies 18 months and older. Choose French green lentils. Buy them dry, and soak them overnight before cooking for a long time, or buy them cooked and vacuum-packed. **56-57**

**Lettuce:** (see red lettuce) **24-25**

**Mango:** Choose one that is spotless and firm but which gives when you press on it. The color, which ranges from green to orange, specifies the variety and not the fruit's ripeness. Imported from the Americas, Africa, and South-East Asia (varieties from this region taste and smell the best). For babies over 6 months, above all for its vitamin C

and carotenes. **108, 110**

**Maple Syrup:** Canadian "honey." **118-119**

**Melon:** Hydrates, revitalizes, and acts as a diuretic. Rich in water, potassium, sugar, vitamins (C, carotenes), and a whole rage of minerals and trace elements. Starting at 6 months. **42**

**Mint:** A fresh-smelling perennial. Soothing, antispasmodic, aids digestion. **42, 64-65, 80-81**

**Mozzarella:** Fresh, soft cheese from southern Italy, made with buffalo cow's milk. Rich in protein and fat. The best comes from Italy's Campania region. For babies over the age of 1. **67**

**Nutmeg:** Sweet spice to be grated or used in powder form. **66-67**

**Oil:** Olive, corn, and sunflower oils: preferably uncooked, for babies over 6 months. Peanut oil: not before 18 months (allergy risk). All of these are rich in calories, vitamin E, and essential fatty acids, which are good for baby's nervous system.

**Onion:** Rich in carbohydrates, mineral salts, carotenes, and B vitamins. This vegetable has antibacterial properties. **24-25, 27, 32-33, 34, 35, 36-37, 38, 40-41, 46-47, 48-49, 54-55, 58-59, 62-63, 82-83, 84-85**

**Orange:** Starting at 4 months, for their vitamin C content, plus their carotenes, vitamin B9, and soft fibers. **116**

**Papaya:** Famous in Tahiti for helping children to digest. Researchers sing its praises for helping to protect the body in other ways. Choose one that is soft. Starting at 4 months. **110**

**Parmesan:** Among the cheeses the most rich in calcium and phosphorus. Starting at 1 year. **72-73**

**Passion Fruit:** Vitamin C and carotenes. Choose one that is round and plump with smooth, shiny skin. For babies over 8 months. **110, 122-123**

**Pasta:** Carbohydrates, protein, and calories. Baby can eat vermicelli or alphabet soup at 6 months and "grown-up pasta" at 8 months. **67**

**Peach:** One of the first fruits you can give to the little ones. One of the most fragile, as well. Thirst quenching, sweet, and full of vitamins (A) and soft fiber (if just ripe). Choose ones that are soft to the touch, but don't press so hard as to bruise them. Or buy them still slightly hard and let them ripen at room temperature away from other fruit. Prepare them immediately before serving. **20-21, 105**

**Pear:** A summer, fall, and even winter fruit to be handled with care to avoid bruising. Cut it right before serving so that it doesn't turn brown. Refreshing and hydrating, this fruit contains soft fibers and several types of sugar, such as sorbitol, which stimulates digestion. Good for babies starting at 4 months. Continues to ripen after picking. **21, 48-49, 105**

**Peas, "fresh from the garden":** From May to July in markets. Choose them smooth, shiny, plump, and fresh. Tender (soft fiber) and sweet (carbohydrates), these little treasures are the richest in protein of all the green vegetables. Fresh (organic) or frozen, babies can enjoy these in soups from 4 months and as a purée from 6-8 months. But no whole peas before 3 years old to avoid swallowing down the "wrong tube"! **32-33, 46-47**

**Pecan: .** Very nutritious and full of calories. Rich in fatty acids, protein, minerals, trace elements, and vitamins (B1, B2, B3, and E). Good for babies over 18 months if ground very fine. **120**

**Pineapple:** One of the most vitamin-rich fruits. Stimulates digestion thanks to an enzyme called bromelain. Can be found fresh all year round. Choose one with very green leaves and an "air shipped" label, which guarantees that it was quickly transported from the tropics. Baby can start enjoying well-blended pineapple at 8 months. **110**

**Pine Nut:** Seed of the pine tree, whose subtle flavor has been enjoyed around the world since ancient times. Rich in protein and calories, it contains an oil that is reputedly good for intellectual stimulation. **62-63**

**Plum and Mirabelle:** Starting from 4 months in small quantities. Contain a good amount of minerals and trace elements. Help purify the body (sorbitol and fiber). When picked ripe, they are covered with a white film. **122-123**

**Pork:** Adds flavor to a "grown-up" dish. Otherwise, wait until age 4 (as long as possible for cooked pork meats), except for lean boiled ham, which is good for babies over 5-6 months. **82-83**

**Potato:** Mashed: not before 8 months because of its fiber content. Wait 18 months for fries and potato chips. It is much richer than all other vegetables in carbohydrates (including starch) and contains a good range of minerals, trace elements, and vitamin C (yup!), especially when freshly harvested, starting in March with new potatoes and until the end of July. **22, 24-25, 26, 34, 35, 38, 46-47, 48-49, 50-51, 54-55, 70-71, 78-79, 82-83, 84-85, 86-87, 94-95**

**Quince:** The pectin in this fruit helps alleviate intestinal problems, just like carrots, but in recipes that are sweet (and cooked). Good for baby starting at 4 months. **104, 116**

**Radish:** Rich in mineral salts and a good amount of vitamin C. Choose small and firm. **46-47**

**Raspberry:** Very fragile! Pick them yourself or buy them firm, fragrant, and with a frosted appearance. Enjoy this fruit, rich in vitamins A and C, and fiber, immediately after purchase. For babies over 6 months. **115, 123**

**Red lettuce:** Colorful lettuce with tight leaves (tinged with red), a crunchy, firm center, and a sweet taste. This vegetable is rich in water, fiber, minerals, trace elements, and vitamins. **24-25**

**Rhubarb:** An astringent with plenty of dietary fiber. Wait until baby is 1 year old. **114**

**Ricotta:** Cheese made from goat or sheep's milk and an integral part of the traditional cuisine of Italy's Campania region. Used in many desserts, like the Pasteria at Easter from Naples. **675**

**Rosemary:** Tonic and stimulating. **58-59**

**Sage:** A slightly bitter Mediterranean plant. Aids digestion and acts as a stimulant. **50-51**

**Salmon:** A migratory fish that is born in fresh-water, migrates to the ocean, and returns upstream in fresh water rivers to reproduce. Wild salmon less than 3 years old from Scotland and Scandinavia is a true delicacy. This "cold water fish" is rich in essential fatty acids and vitamins A and D, which help the body to assimilate the calcium and phosphorus it contains. Good for babies over the age of 1. **94-95**

**Salsify:** Carbohydrates, fibers. After 18 months. **48-49**

**Savory:** A sweet, citrus-scented Mediterranean plant. **54-55**

**Scallops:** Protein, vitamin C, phosphorus, iodine, and zinc. After 18 months. **100-101**

**Sea Bass:** It's called "Atlantic Sea Bass" when fished in Brittany but just a "sea bass" when it comes from the Mediterranean. Lean fish, rich in protein, iodine and fluoride. From 5-6 months. **90-91**

**Shallots:** The pink skinned variety has a sweeter taste. "New" shallots arrive in July. Choose firm shallots with tight skin. **68, 100-101**

**Sherry Vinegar:** Vinegar made with sherry from Andalusia. Its warm, oak flavor comes from the oak barrels in which the wine is fermented for six or more years. **40-41**

**Shrimp:** Protein, iodine, zinc, and vitamin C! Buy precooked (except when fresh from the sea), firm, and without a fishy smell. For children over 2. **44**

**Smoked Country Bacon:** Exceptionally to add flavor to a "grown-up" dish. **74-75**

**Smoked Ham:** Simply to add flavor to a "grown-up" dish. **84-85**

**Sole:** A mild flavored, lean white fish, very rich in calcium, phosphorus, iodine, and fluoride. Ideal for baby starting at 5-6 months. Buy it extremely fresh, with a pearly-white color, and serve it cooked through (it will be drier if bought frozen). **96-97**



**Spinach:** High in iron, fiber, mineral salts (potassium, calcium and magnesium), trace elements (fluoride), and vitamins (C, K, B9). Spinach is safe for babies 5-6 months old if it is garden-grown or organic. Otherwise, wait till baby is at least a year old (too many nitrates in the cooking water is not good for young babies). This leafy green can be found fresh all year round (although it does not withstand the summer heat very well). Choose young leaves that are fresh, tender, shiny, and deep green in color. Wash and keep in the refrigerator in a towel, but eat them as soon as they are cooked **34, 36-37, 66-67, 96-97**

**Strawberry:** Choose strawberries that are ripe and bright in color with no bruises. Eat them quickly, without placing them in the refrigerator or near other fruits. They are sweet (fructose) and have a balance of vitamins (C, carotene) and minerals. This fruit contains salicylic acid (aspirin, yes!), which is where it gets its medicinal properties. However, they do give off histamines, which is why people are often allergic to them. Introduce this sweet treat to baby's diet little by little starting at 5-6 months. **20-21, 114-115, 122**

**Sweet Pepper:** Choose the sweeter red ones rather than the green because they contain twice the vitamin C and carotenes. Buy them firm, shiny, smooth, and without spots or bruises. **40-41, 43, 62-63**

Plum

**Swiss Chard:** Easy to grow in the kitchen garden, wonderful to eat. White stem and green leaves. This vegetable with soft fibers is rarely recognized for the carotenes and vitamin C in its leaves, as well as its potassium, calcium and iron. From 5-6 months. **48-49, 94-95**

**Tarragon:** Spice with small leaves and a slight anis flavor that comes out in cooking. **122-123**

**Thyme:** Usually used cooked. Choose a very pungent variety with smaller leaves. Aids digestion. **26, 56-57, 94-95**

**Tomato:** Very ripe, seedless, and cooked tomato flesh is good for babies over 4-6 months, but raw tomatoes should not be eaten by babies under the age of 1. Wait until May to buy tomatoes at their peak in smell, taste, vitamins (a lot of vitamin C!), and minerals. Once bought, store them at room temperature. Cold air robs this red gem of its taste. **27, 40-41, 62-63, 70-71, 78-79, 90-91**

**Turkey:** Protein, phosphorus, potassium, magnesium, and iron. This "chicken of India" was discovered by Christopher Columbus in North America and is on every French table at Christmas and every American menu for Thanksgiving. Babies over 5-6 months old can eat cutlets. Make sure to buy a heritage breed turkey. **74-75**

**Turnip:** For potassium, calcium, carbohydrates and vitamins. A light little spring vegetable. Starting at 18 months. **46-47, 80-81**

sage

**Vanilla:** Sweet-smelling bean from the tropics whose seeds are prized for their delicious flavor. **105**

**Veal:** Lean and tender meat. Veal cutlets can be given to babies at 5-6 months. **86-87**

**Walnut Oil:** **28-29, 68**

**Walnuts and Hazelnuts:** To avoid swallowing down the "wrong tube," don't give these to children under 3, even in powder form and even though they are rich in fat (essential fatty acids), protein, phosphorus and fiber. Fresh walnuts can be bought in the fall. **69**

**Watercress:** Tones and replenishes the body's minerals! With almost as much calcium and vitamin C as parsley, it is one of the richest vegetables in vitamins (B9, carotenes) and minerals. Good for babies around 5-6 months old if it comes from a certified watercress bed that is watered with spring water. But please, no wild watercress, especially for baby! **24-25**

**Watermelon:** Dripping with water, rich in vitamins. Choose one with a rind that is smooth, thick, soft, and homogenous in color, with a small crack by the stem that says that it is ripe for the picking. Good for babies starting at 8 months. **107**

**White Bread:** The crust can be munched on at 10 months but the soft center not until 18 months. Whole-grain bread will have to wait a little longer: 7 years old, the age of reason. Carbohydrates, protein, vitamin B9, fiber, and gluten (watch out for allergies). **32-33, 56-57**

**Wild Strawberry:** This ancestor of commercially grown varieties is very fragile. Pick them in the garden or woods. At the market, make sure not to buy them over-ripe, bruised, or wet. And enjoy them right away. This fruit, rich in vitamins A and C, and fiber, is for babies over 6 months. **114-115**

**Wild Thyme:** Has a subtle flavor. **35**

**Winter Squash:** From 4 months. Extremely rich in potassium, with a very large amount of carotenes. Like its cousin the pumpkin, this vegetable comes from the squash family from North America and has some odd qualities: it can keep the ghosts away, turn into a horse-drawn carriage, or be a Halloween decoration. How to identify it? By the stem and its flat top. **23, 48-49, 72-73**

**Yeast:** Protein, the whole range of B vitamins, and a good amount of calcium. **118-119**

**Yogurt:** Calcium! This fermented milk is valued for its protein and vitamins (B2, B12). Even better: special "just for baby" yogurts, which are made with enriched milk and are specially formulated for children from 1 to 3 years old. Enriched in iron and essential fatty acids **122-123**

**Zucchini:** Brought back from the New World for its beautiful flower (which is edible!) and not considered a vegetable till much later. Zucchini can be found today in markets from May to October. Choose a young, long, and skinny one that is firm, smooth, and uniform in color (dark green). They should be eaten within 48 hours after buying because they dry out very quickly. Light and easy to digest, with soft fibers and a good amount of vitamins and minerals. Good for baby starting at 4 months old. **26, 46-47, 64-65, 80-81**

**Baby is already growing up and is ready to taste flavors and textures other than milk and cereals.**

**Mom is fully investing herself in her role as the attentive mother in order to give her little angel what is best.**

**And in a brand new Babycook.**

**It is well known that steam cooking is far and away the best method of cooking foods, to make certain that all of their valuable nutritional qualities remain intact. Food should be blended right after steaming,** to the consistency that corresponds with your fledgling's stage of development, so as to give him a beakful of food immediately when it is done.

**That deserves a chapter of its own, so that everyone can get familiarized before** becoming comfortable with the equipment, taking liberties with the advice given, and savoring those special parent-child moments when baby eats. Dad is going to participate, too. Don't forget that it was Chef Dad who created these recipes for his son Alphonse!

**Above all, these recipes are extremely easy.**

**The first fruits and vegetables that we will give to baby will be steamed,** and the recipes will respect the ingredients' pure flavors (The Boss of the Applesauce). Later, moms will be able to refine the recipes little by little (Carrot Soup, Tomato Fondue), enhance them over time (Pumpkin Velouté, Fork-Smashed Zucchini), couple them with veggies from the same family (from watercress to red lettuce), and make them much more sophisticated for special days (Artichoke, Leaf by Leaf).

**The next step is to use the blender to pulse together the food in order to achieve the desired consistency, depending on baby's stage of development...because the little guy is going to get big!** Thin soups and veloutés to be drunk from the baby bottle? 3 pulses. Purée or compote when baby is ready to use a spoon? 2 pulses. The consistency of marmalade or caviar (!) when baby's first chompers come in? 1 pulse. And the pulse will become shorter as the little guy starts to chew little bits.



**Ingredients are chosen** by following the main principles of child nutrition, with a few pieces of advice to help you pick or buy them when they are at the peak of freshness.

**At first, the flavors are sweet. We will refine them** a tiny bit at around age 1 and a tad more when baby's tastes become clearer, around 18 months as a general rule. But we do see precocious babies who love vinegar (balsamic to start because it is the sweetest) and grains of fleur de sel, even if it is not at all recommended before the age of one, and only in very small amounts even then.

**And these "Our First Time" recipes can be adapted over time, because if baby likes them, he will for many years to come.**

19

# Our First Time

Mom's Advice:

*These are thirst quenching summer desserts and are very important if your baby does not like to drink water. Mixing some tasty cooking juices with water is a great way to get baby to drink more.*



**4 months and up**

# The Boss of the Applesauce

[ **10 to 15 min**

**Useful Utensils**

Cutting board
Paring knife
2 large glasses (or bottles)

**Down to Basics**

Seasonal fruit mixes, to be made up immediately before feeding them to baby. To be served lukewarm, cool, or even chilled (for babies over 1, because baby will love these recipes for a long time!). Add a little sugar, if need be, and keep the cooking juices in a cool place for snack time.

## Peach-Pear Compote

**Grocery list for a 4 month old baby...**

[ **at the market** 2 nicely colored peaches
1 Bartlett pear

[ **at the grocery store** A sprinkling of sugar

**This recipe's good points:**

*Peaches and pears are perfect for little ones. They are refreshing, hydrating, light, and full of vitamins and soft fibers. And, in addition to the sugar found in peaches, the sorbitol in pears stimulates digestion. But both of these fruits are fragile, so handle them with care and prepare them at the last minute.*

### Here we go!

[ Thoroughly rinse the fruit. Peel the pear, cut it into four pieces, and remove the core and seeds. Cut the flesh into pieces and place them directly into the steamer basket. Run the back edge of the paring knife over the skin of the peaches so that the skins come off easily (an expert's technique!). Peel the peaches, cut them in half, and pit them. Cut the flesh into pieces and place them in the steamer basket. Cook them for 5 minutes (water level 1). Keep the cooking juices in a glass. Transfer the fruit to the blending bowl and pulse once. Taste and, if necessary, sprinkle with a bit of sugar. Serve while still a lukewarm.

## Strawberry-Pear Compote

**This recipe's good points:**

*Strawberries are chock-full of fructose and vitamin C when ripe (bright red with a strong scent). But the risk of allergies because of their histamine content requires parents to wait 5 or 6 months before introducing them slowly but surely into baby's diet. Pears are rich in water, sugar, and vitamins, which makes these two fruits a perfect "pear"!*

**Grocery list for a 6 month old baby...**

**[ at the market** 1/2 pear (Comice pears in the winter/spring, Bartlett in the summer)
1/2 pint strawberries (1 cup whole berries)

**[ at the grocery store** A sprinkling of brown sugar

**...and for a 1 year old**

1 whole pear
1 pint strawberries (2 cups whole berries)
(...and brown sugar)



Chef Dad's Advice:

*Why Bartlett pears in summer? Because they are juicy, tender, sweet smelling, and perfect for compotes and marmalades, or smashed with a fork. And in the spring? Choose Comice pears, which are sweet and stay good longer.*

### Here we go!

[ Peel the pear, cut it into quarters, and remove the core and the seeds. Place the quarters in the steamer basket. Rinse the strawberries in a strainer with cold water. Then dry and stem them. Add them to the steamer basket. Cook them for 10 minutes (water level 2). Keep the cooking juices in a glass. Transfer the fruit to the blending bowl and pulse twice to obtain a light and liquid compote.

[ Taste and carefully add sugar until the compote is flavorful, without overpowering the taste of the fruit.

## Strawberry-Banana Compote

**This recipe's good points:**

*A good pair! Dense, soft, and sweet (the more yellow and spotted, the sweeter), bananas are a wonderful source of potassium and magnesium. Light and revitalizing, strawberries are jam-packed with fructose and vitamin C – but don't forget to watch out for allergic reactions*

**Grocery list for a 6 month old baby...**

**[ at the market** 1/2 ripe banana
1/2 pint strawberries
(1 cup whole berries)

**[ at the grocery store** A sprinkling of sugar

**...and for a 1 year old**

1 whole banana
1 pint strawberries (2.5 cups whole berries)
(...and the sugar)

### Here we go!

[ Peel the banana. Cut half of the banana (for babies up to 12 months old) or the whole banana (for babies over 1-year-old) into large pieces. Place them in the steamer basket. Rinse the strawberries in a strainer under running water. Then dry and stem them. Add them to the steamer basket. Cook everything for 10 minutes (water level 2).

[ Pour the cooking juices into a glass. Transfer the fruit to the blending bowl. Pulse 2 or 3 times to mix the fruit together. Add the cooking juices (in small quantities) between each pulse, until you obtain a light compote of the desired consistency. Taste and, if necessary, add a bit of sugar.

Chef Dad's Advice:

*Carrots are the first vegetable that we can give to babies, starting at 4 months old, to introduce them to a more diverse diet. This is one of the first recipes that I made for Alphonse. He took to it right away.*



**4 months and up**

# Carrot Soup

[ 20 min

**Useful Utensils**

Cutting board
Vegetable peeler
Paring knife

**Grocery list for a 4 month old baby...**

**[ at the market** 1 carrot
1 small Yukon Gold potato

**[ at the grocery store** 1 pat butter
(for babies 6 months and up)

**...and for a 1 year old**

**[ at the market** 2 carrots

**[ at the grocery store** 1 small pinch salt
1 pat butter
...and maybe a few ice cubes

**This recipe's good points:**

*Carrots! In France, we are born liking them and we remain faithful to them for life, both for their bright color and sweet taste. And it's a good thing, because the beta carotene they contain gives you beautiful skin and rosy cheeks (and a rosy bottom!), and their soft fibers aid digestion. Make sure to buy them straight from the garden, or organic (so that they contain as few nitrates as possible). Potatoes add starch, minerals, and vitamins. And butter is an excellent source of A vitamins when eaten raw.*

## Here we go!

### For little ones from 4 months to 1 year

[ Thoroughly wash the carrot and potato. Peel them with the vegetable peeler and wash them again. Cut the carrot into small slices (watch your fingers!), dice the potato, and cook them for 15 minutes (water level 3) in the steamer basket. Throw the cooking juices away. Transfer the vegetables to the blending bowl. Pulse 3 times. Add a small amount of slightly mineralized water between each pulse, until you obtain a smooth consistency that is thin enough to be drunk from a baby bottle. Make it a bit thicker later on, when baby starts learning to eat from a spoon.

### For babies over 1 year old

[ Make sure that the butter is hard. If not, place it on top of a few ice cubes to cool. Forget about the potato! Prepare the carrots as above, but sprinkle them with a bit of salt before cooking them. Throw the cooking juices away and proceed as above with the blender until you obtain the desired thin consistency. Pour the velouté into baby's bowl. Cut the butter into little pieces and sprinkle it on the mixture, so baby will have the pleasure of seeing "little suns" melt on an orange-colored sky.

Chef Dad's Advice:

*For older babies, I mix crunchy and creamy by sprinkling the velouté with a few cubes of pumpkin (2 oz). When preparing the soup, I set a few raw pieces aside, cook them in a frying pan with a tiny bit of olive oil, without letting them brown, and dry them off on a piece of paper towel.*



4 months and up

# Pumpkin Velouté

[ **20 to 25 min**

## Useful Utensils

1 bowl
Tablespoon
Cutting board
Paring knife
...and for babies over 8 months
Another bowl
Small frying pan (if necessary)
Paper towel (if necessary)

**This recipe's good points:**

*Pumpkin is a big hit early on because it is tender and sweet. So much the better! It is recommended for babies 4 months and up because of its abundance of potassium, iron, magnesium, soft fibers, and beta carotene (good growth, good vision), which gives it its sunny color. The egg yolk makes a good mate, with its high-quality proteins, phosphorus, and vitamin content (especially B vitamins).*

**Grocery list for a 4 to 12 month old baby...**

[ **at the market**
3.5 oz pumpkin (= 1 small slice) for a 4 month old
5.5 oz pumpkin (= 1 medium slice) for an 8 month old
7 oz pumpkin (= 1 large slice) for a 1 year old

...with, at 4 months: 2 tablespoons prepared baby formula
...plus, at 8 months: 1 farm-fresh egg yolk from a free-range chicken
1 small pat butter

**...adding the following for a 1 year old**

[ **at the grocery store**
2 tablespoons prepared milk-based pediatric nutritional supplement (instead of the prepared formula)
1 tablespoon olive oil
1 tiny pinch salt
1/4 turn of the pepper mill (white pepper)

## Here we go!

[ Thoroughly wash the pumpkin. Remove the rind and seeds. Dice the flesh and cook it for 15 minutes (water level 3) in the steamer basket. Pour the cooking juice into a bowl.

[ **For babies 4 to 8 months old:** Transfer the cooked flesh to the blending bowl. Add the milk. Blend the ingrecients (3 pulses) to obtain a perfect velouté. If necessary, add a bit of cooking juice between pulses until you obtain a consistency that is thin enough to be drunk from a baby bottle.

[ **For babies 8 to 10 months old:** Before blending, add to the milk an egg yolk and a small pat of butter. Proceed as above.

[ **For babies 1 year and up:** Season the velouté with a bit of salt (and a very tiny bit of pepper for 2-3 year old children), pour it into a bowl, and decorate it with thin drizzle of olive oil.

Chef Dad's Advice:

*If, for older babies, you would prefer to make a watercress purée, blend with the least amount of water possible. Then mix with a spoonful of crème fraîche and butter right before serving.*



6 months and up

# Watercress Velouté...

[ **15** min

**Useful Utensils**

Large bowl
Paring knife
Vegetable peeler
Cutting board
Chinois

**Grocery list for a 6 month old baby...**

**[ at the market**

1/2 bunch watercress
1/2 baking potato

**[ at the grocery store**

1 Tbsp vinegar (to wash the watercress)
1 Tbsp prepared baby formula

**...and for a 1 year old**

[ **take away** the milk

**[ add**

1/4 white onion
And for the purée (if necessary):
1 Tbsp thick crème fraîche
1 small pat butter

## Here we go!

### For little ones from 6 to 12 months

[ Soak the watercress, with the top of the bunch facing down, in a large bowl of vinegar water. Then rinse it several times in running water, shaking the bunch between each rinse. Cut the tops off with a knife, leaving a little bit of the stem (1 inch). Thoroughly wash the potato, peel it with a vegetable peeler, and wash it again. Cut half of the potato into smaller pieces. Cook the chopped potato for 10 minutes (water level 2) in the steamer basket. Throw the cooking juices away.

[ Transfer the cooked vegetables to the blending bowl. Pulse 3 times. Add the milk before the 2nd pulse and a small amount of slightly mineralized water before the 3rd pulse if you desire a consistency that is thin enough to be drunk from a baby bottle.

### For babies 1 year and up

[ Peel the onion. Chop 1/4 of the onion into small pieces and add them to the steamer basket.

[ When the cooked vegetables are in the blending bowl, pulse 3 times. Add a small amount of slightly mineralized water (but no milk) between each pulse, to obtain a velouté. Strain the mixture through the Chinois to obtain a perfectly thin velouté.

**This recipe's good points:**

*Watercress is only to be eaten if it comes from a certified watercress bed that is watered with spring water. This is one of the vegetables richest in vitamins (B9, or folic acid, and carotenes) and minerals (especially calcium).*

*Red lettuce is a small leafy vegetable that is crunchy, sweet, rich in water, and stuffed with numerous micronutrients.*

25

**4 months and up**

# ...and Red Lettuce Milk

[ **This recipe is an adaptation of a "grown-up" recipe for infants,** although many variations will remain on the menu for a long time, of watercress to the more tender red lettuce (or small green leaf lettuce).

[ Throw the bigger leaves and core away. Keep only the lettuce heart. Wash the lettuce and a small Yukon Gold potato. Cut them into pieces. Cook them for 10 minutes (water level 2) in the steamer basket. Throw away the cooking juices.

[ Transfer the vegetables to the blending bowl. Into the blending bowl, pour 5 tablespoons of prepared baby formula (for babies 12 months and younger) or, for older babies, prepared milk-based pediatric nutritional supplement or 1 tablespoon of crème fraîche. Add 1 sprig of chervil that has been rinsed and cut up with scissors.

[ Blend: 2 to 3 pulses, depending on the desired consistency. The mixture should be light and thin enough to be drunk from a baby bottle, if desired.

Mom serves *the watercress velouté with a whiting filet, steam-cooked for 5 minutes (water level 1).*

Chef Dad's Advice:
*For babies over 1 year old, emphasize the Mediterranean flavor of this dish. Make an herb sachet out of cloth and fill it with 3 or 4 coriander seeds, thyme, and no more than 1 bay leaf. Tie it up and place it in the steamer basket before cooking.*



**6 months and up**

# Fork-Smashed Zucchini

[ 15 min

**Useful Utensils**

Cutting board
Paring knife
Scissors
Fork

And for babies over the age of 1:
Small piece of fabric (cheesecloth, linen, burlap)
6 inches kitchen twine

**This recipe's good points:**

*A good range of vitamins and a good mix of minerals! The zucchini, whose nutritional value was discovered very late, is easily digestible, low in calories, full of soft fiber, and good for babies 4 months and older. Parsley is a good source of calcium, as are potatoes, whose starch thickens the dish.*

**Grocery list for a 6 to 12 month old baby...**

**[ at the market** 1 small zucchini
1 small Yukon Gold potato
1 sprig flat-leaf parsley

**[ at the grocery store** 1 Tbsp prepared baby formula (up to 8 months) ...or 1 thin drizzle of olive oil (after 8 months)

**[ at the butcher's** 1 thin slice lean boiled ham (shoulder), starting at 8 months

**...and for a 1 year old**

**[ at the market, add** a second zucchini of similar size
1 bay leaf
3 or 4 thyme leaves
3 or 4 coriander seeds

## Here we go!

[ Cut off the ends of the zucchini. Thoroughly wash it under running water, because the skin will be left on to add color to the dish. Cut it into 4 pieces lengthwise. Remove any seeds with a knife. Cut the quarters into smaller pieces. Rinse the potato under running water, peel it with the vegetable peeler, wash it again, and cut it into pieces. Place the vegetables into the steamer basket. Cook them for exactly 10 minutes (water level 2) so that the zucchini keeps its green color. While they are cooking, wash and dry the parsley. Strip the leaves off the stem and finely cut them with scissors. Throw the cooking juices away.

[ **For 6 to 8 month olds:** Transfer the vegetables to the blending bowl with the parsley. Pulse 2 or 3 times, adding a little milk between each pulse, until the desired consistency is obtained.

[ **From 8 months on:** Bye-bye blending bowl and milk! Scatter the raw parsley and cooked zucchini and potatoes on a plate. Smash them with a fork and drizzle them with a bit of olive oil. Serve with lean boiled-ham (from the shoulder, which is the most tender) that has been cut into very thin slices (almost shredded) by your butcher.

Chef Dad's Pasta:

*I mix 1 ounce of semi-fresh goat cheese with 1/4 cup of tomato fondue and pulse once. Then I add 1 basil leaf and pulse once more. I serve the resulting sauce with pasta, which makes for a delicious, healthy, and well-balanced dish.*

**6-8 months and up**

# Tomato Fondue "Our Way"

[ 15 min

### Useful Utensils

Small mixing bowl
Small saucepan
Cutting board
Paring knife
Serrated knife
Slotted spoon
Plastic wrap

**This recipe's good points:**

*Tomatoes are light, thirst-quenching, rich in vitamins, minerals, and trace elements. When cooked, very ripe, skinless, and seedless (because they contain irritants), they are good for babies over 4 months in soups and later in fondues. Raw, firm, and skinless tomatoes (always!) are reserved for babies over one.*

**Grocery list for a 6 month old baby**

**[ at the market**
1 tomato
2 basil leaves (4 leaves for children over 1 year old)
plus, for children over 1 year old: 1/4 green onion
1/2 clove new garlic
...and 1 beefsteak tomato, for special days

**[ at the grocery store**
1 drizzle olive oil
1/2 tsp tomato paste (1 tsp for 1 year olds)
...and a few ice cubes (to peel the tomato) plus, for children over 1 year old: 1 tiny pinch salt
a few grains of fleur de sel
1/4 turn of the pepper mill (white pepper)

## Here we go!

[ Fill the mixing bowl with cold water and ice cubes. Boil water in the saucepan. Clean the basil under running water, strip the leaves from the stem, and rip the leaves into small pieces.

[ **For little ones from 6 to 12 months:** Cut out the tomato stem with a knife. Plunge the tomato in the boiling water for 20 seconds and then place it in the cold water. Dry it and peel the skin off. Child's play! Cut the tomato in half, remove the seeds (easiest with the fingers) and place it in the steamer basket. Cook for 10 minutes (water level 2). Throw the cooking juices away. Transfer the tomato to the blending bowl. Add the tomato paste to brighten the color. Pulse once. Add the basil and pulse again. The resulting mixture will be slightly grainy. Pour into a bowl, drizzle with a bit of olive oil, and feed to your little one.

[ **For babies over 1 year old...** Remove the green onion's outer layer. Cut 1/4 of the green onion and 1/2 of the garlic clove into thin slices. Place them in the steamer basket with the tomato. Proceed as above. Use the basil to garnish the cooked fondue. Cool the dish, covered with plastic wrap, in the refrigerator for several minutes. Lightly salt it before serving.

[ **...and a "special day" tomato extravaganza variation:** Spread the fondue in thin layers over thin slices of a sweet and juicy Beefsteak tomato (peeled). Cut the tomato with a serrated knife and sprinkle the slices with a few grains of fleur de sel and a pinch of white pepper.

**Mom's Advice:**

*When this vegetable is out of season, frozen artichoke hearts are a good replacement.*

**4 months and up**

# My First Artichoke



**Useful Utensils**

Cutting board
Paring knife
Teaspoon

[ 20 min (+ 5 min if necessary)

**Grocery list for a 4 month old baby...**

1 artichoke
1 Tbsp prepared baby formula

**...and for an 8 month old baby**

1 artichoke
and 1 drizzle olive oil
instead of the prepared baby formula

**Grocery list for a 1 year old child**
(see page 29)

[ **at the market** 2 artichokes
1/4 lemon
2 Tbsp flour

[ **at the grocery store** 1 drizzle walnut oil

**This recipe's good points:**

*The evolving artichoke: velouté in a bottle, and purée for the little ones without chompers, served in a bowl to those with growing appetites, and decorated with artichoke leaves.*

*This member of the thistle family is extremely rich in minerals. It also contains a type of sugar, inuline, which helps the body to assimilate these minerals, is good for a balanced intestinal flora, and gives the veggie its sweet taste, which is enjoyed even by very young children.*

## Here we go!

[ **For little ones from 4 months to 8 months:** Wash the artichoke under running water. Vigorously shake it off, with the head facing down so as get rid of any dirt. Peel off the first few leaves and break the stem by hand (instead of cutting it) to pull out all of the artichoke's hard fibers. Cut the raw artichoke around the bottom. Remove the choke with a teaspoon and cut the heart into big pieces. Cook the pieces for 15 minutes (water level 3) in the steamer basket. Throw the cooking juices away. Transfer the pieces to the blending bowl. Pulse 3 times, adding a little milk between each pulse to obtain a velouté that is thin enough to be drunk from a bottle; or pulse only twice, and add a little milk or slightly mineralized water between pulses to obtain a purée that can be eaten with a spoon. Pulse only once for a "big kid's" purée with little chunks.

[ **For little ones from 8 to 12 months:** Mix by pulsing once without milk or water. Decorate the dish with a little drizzle of olive oil and the little guy will open wide!

Chef Dad's recipe for babies over 1 year old

# Artichoke, Leaf by Leaf

[ **On special days, I make this recipe complete** by cooking a second whole artichoke (washed, with the stem broken by hand) in a white court-bouillon. I heat water in a pot with 2 tablespoons of flour and the juice of 1/4 of a lemon. I place the artichoke in the pot when the water begins to boil and let it cook for 20 minutes. While it is cooking, I prepare artichoke purée with the Babycook. Once the artichoke is finished cooking in the court bouillon, I remove all of the leaves around the bottom (and I meant "around"). I cut the artichoke around the bottom and remove all of the tender leaves from the center. Then I remove the choke with a teaspoon.

[ **I fill the artichoke heart with the artichoke purée** and arrange a dozen or so of the tender leaves around it. I drizzle the dish with a small amount of walnut oil. And the whole family applauds...Alphonse, too!

**Green vegetables and fine herbs from the garden. Mediterranean vegetables and the winter market. Chef Dad casts his net wide! His recipes highlight each and every flavor, and allow "little sprouts" to discover these tastes in order to be able to identify, better recognize them (even in seasonal dishes that have been puréed), and savor them so as to better appreciate and like them.**

**Fresh vegetables are so rich in vitamins, minerals, and trace elements** that they, along with fruits, are the first food items to become a part of baby's diet after milk. In general, wait until baby is 4 months old before introducing them. After that they will follow him every step of his merry way.

**Because the body cannot make its own vitamins, minerals, or trace elements, it must receive a balanced dose of these daily** by way of the diet. And so balance is born out of variety, the freshness of the produce used, as well as the delicate preparation. Preparation is of the utmost importance because a good amount of the vitamins (C and B9, in particular) found in fresh produce evaporate into thin air in the 24 hours after produce is picked, and others disappear in water or in cooking juices. And drinking cooking juices is not always recommended because they often contain high levels of nitrates (for carrots which are not organic or from the garden, and especially for spinach).

**Fresh vegetables should be chosen very fresh and young** (soft fibers) but firm and colorful (or frozen), with the label "certified organic," if possible. Wash them carefully (because of pesticides) but do not let them soak. And eat them as soon as possible..

**So called "greens"** (which can be as red as a tomato!) all contain large amounts of water and fiber (soft fibers in asparagus and leeks, and effective fiber in spinach), in addition to mineral salts (potassium and magnesium, which reinforce calcium's effect on the body), trace elements (iron, copper, etc.), and vitamins (which are fragile!) such as carotenes, especially in vegetables the color of the sun (peppers, pumpkin). They contain little protein and no fat or calories, except for avocados! They also only contain very few carbohydrates, except for artichokes, beets, peas and salsify.

**Fine herbs** (parsley, chervil, basil, tarragon, and chives) are a fresh source of calcium and vitamin K.

**Seasonings** (thyme and wild thyme, bay leaves, rosemary, savory, and sage) and **sweet spices** (nutmeg, cloves, curry, etc.) are used in tiny amounts to season or bring out a dish's taste.

**Garlic and onions** are as valuable in cooking as they are healthy, because of their rich taste and richness in nutrients.

**During the winter months, legumes provide the body with plant proteins and dense carbohydrates** comparable to those found in pasta and rice. They are also rich in B vitamins, mineral salts, and fiber, as well.



**And as for the potato, it is a kitchen garden in and of itself...**

# 31 From the Kitchen Garden

32

Mom's Advice:
*For connoisseurs, serve this purée with a scrambled egg topped with a chopped coriander leaf (to be added at the last moment)… and watch them dig in!*

From the Kitchen Garden

6 months and up

# Mom and Baby, Two Peas in a Pod

Spring

[ 20 min

**Useful Utensils**

Cutting board
Paring knife
Bowl
Chinois

**Grocery list for a 6 month old baby…**

10 garden peapods
1 Tbsp prepared baby formula

**…and for a 1 year old**

[ **at the market** 15 garden peapods
1/2 green onion

[ **at the grocery store** 1 small pat salted butter
1 or 2 croutons

## This recipe's good points:

*Peas are so sweet and tender that baby will like them right away, which makes moms happy because they are rich in carbohydrates (energy), protein (for building a strong body), and fiber (intestinal transit). Fresh (and organic!) or frozen, peas can be given to baby in soups starting at 4 months and in purées starting at 6-8 months. But no whole peas before age 3, so that they don't take a trip down the "wrong tube!"*

## Here we go!

[ **For little ones from 6 to 12 months:** Wash the pods. Shell half of the peas and leave the rest. Place all of the shelled and unshelled peas in the steamer basket. Cook for 15 minutes (water level 3). Pour the cooking juices into a bowl. Transfer the cooked peas to the blending bowl. Blend to obtain a smooth consistency (2 pulses), adding the milk between the first and second pulse.

[ **For babies 1 year and up:** Prepare the peas as above. Set aside 3 or 4 raw peas for decoration. Peel the onion, cut it in half, and slice half of it thinly. Add it to the steamer basket. Once the vegetables are cooked, pour the cooking juices into a bowl, and transfer the cooked vegetables to the blending bowl. Pulse twice to obtain a smooth consistency, adding some of the cooking juices between the first and second pulse. If you would like to turn this purée into a delicious velouté, pulse a third time and add more of the cooking juices to obtain a liquid, homogenous consistency. Strain the mixture through the Chinois to obtain a perfectly thin velouté and place in the refrigerator for 10 minutes so that it keeps its pretty green color…

Chef Dad's Advice:

*To decorate the purée for older babies, make a thin crostini out of toasted stale bread and butter it with salted butter. Peel 3 or 4 raw peas, and cut them into 4 pieces each (really!). Sprinkle them on the crostini and place this "little boat" on the edge of the plate.*

33

On Market Day

12 months and up

# Spring Velouté

[ **This healthy velouté is made with** 1.75 oz of each of the following veggies: shelled fresh peas, spring carrots, thin French-style green beans, and fava beans. Rinse them all under running water. Shell the peas and the fava beans (remove their skins too; see "Fava Bean Purée"). Snap off the ends of the green beans. Peel the carrot and cut it into thin slices.

[ Steam cook them all for 15 minutes (water level 3). Throw the cooking juices away and transfer the vegetables to the blending bowl. Pulse 3 times, adding a small amount of slightly mineralized water between each pulse to obtain a liquid velouté. Season to taste with a bit of salt, and when baby is older, a bit of white pepper.

[ Pour into a bowl and place a small pat of butter in the middle, which will melt into a little halo.

Chef Dad's Advice:
On special days, I crown this dish with 3 or 4 little broccoli florets that have been cooked "English-style" (blanched for 20 seconds in boiling salted water) and are tender to munch on.



6 months and up

# Broccoli Bouillon

[ 10 to 15 min

**Useful Utensils**

Cutting board
Paring knife
Whisk
Bowl

**Grocery list for a 6 month old baby...**

1/2 broccoli head
1 small Yukon Gold potato
1 Tbsp prepared baby formula

**...and for a 1 year old**

**[ at the market** 1/2 broccoli head
1/2 green onion
3 or 4 spinach leaves

**[ at the grocery store** 1 thin drizzle olive oil
1 Tbsp heavy cream
1 pinch salt (for older babies)

## This recipe's good points:

*Broccoli is the king of vitamin C! And it's full of vitamin A pro-vitamins as well. It is light, easily digestible, and recommended for babies 4 months and up. For younger babies, pair it with potatoes for their richness in complex sugars. For older babies, mix it with spinach, a leafy green that is loaded with vitamins A, B9 and K, calcium, and effective fibers, and turns the bouillon a beautiful green color.*

## Here we go!

[ **For little ones from 6 to 12 months:** Wash the broccoli under running water. Cut off 2 or 3 nice-looking florets with 1-inch stems. Cook them in the steamer basket for 5 minutes (water level 1). Throw the cooking juices away. Transfer the cooked broccoli to the blending bowl. Pulse once. Add the formula. Pulse once more. Feed this bouillon to baby with a baby spoon. To serve it in a bottle, thin it with a small amount of slightly mineralized water and pulse once more.

[ **For babies 1 year and older:** Prepare 3 or 4 broccoli florets as above. Remove the green onion's outer layer and thinly slice half of the white part. Cook the broccoli and onion in the steamer basket for 5 minutes (water level 1). While they are cooking, thoroughly rinse the spinach leaves and stem them. Throw the cooking juices away. Transfer the broccoli and onions to the blending bowl. Add the spinach and a thin drizzle of olive oil. Pulse once. Add a small amount of slightly mineralized water. Pulse again to obtain a delicious velouté. Lightly beat the cream in a bowl with a whisk. Pour the velouté in a bowl, spoon a cloud of whipped cream into the middle, and hear the applause.

6 months and up

# Thyme for Green Bean Purée



[ 15 min

**Useful Utensils**

Cutting board
Vegetable peeler
Paring knife
Bowl

**Grocery list for a 6 month old baby...**

**[ at the market** 1/3 cup (1.5 oz) thin French-style green beans
1/2 baking potato
1 small sprig wild thyme

**...and for a 1 year old**

**[ at the market** 2/3 cup (3 oz) thin French-style green beans
1/4 green onion
1/2 baking potato
1 sprig wild thyme

**[ at the grocery store** 1 thin drizzle olive oil

## This recipe's good points:

*Green beans provide baby with a generous amount of minerals (potassium, magnesium, calcium, sulfur, iron, etc.), vitamins (C, A, and B9 or folic acid, among others), and soft fiber. All that and they are easy on the digestive system, even at an early age.*

*And the aroma of wild thyme...from the fields where wild rabbits play!*

Chef
Dad's Advice:
*For the "grown-up menu," green bean purée goes best with ham, poultry, and fish. Serve it alone or with another purée to add color and flavor.*

## Here we go!

### For little ones from 6 to 12 months:

[ Wash the green beans and snap off their ends. Rinse the potato under running water, peel it with the vegetable peeler, and wash it again before cutting half of it into pieces. Wash the wild thyme. Place it in the steamer basket with the chopped potato and cook for 10 minutes (water level 2).

[ Collect the cooking juices in a bowl. Transfer the steamer basket contents to the blending bowl. Pulse twice, adding a small amount of cooking juices between the pulses in order to obtain the desired consistency.

### For babies 1 year and up:

[ Before cooking, remove the green onion's outer layer and thinly slice the white part. Add it to the other vegetables.

[ Before blending, drizzle a small amount of olive oil into the blending bowl. This intensifies the taste of the green beans while complimenting the flavor of the wild thyme.

Chef Dad's Advice:
*I set aside 2 raw asparagus tips, which I thinly slice with a mandoline. I garnish the velouté with the sliced asparagus before serving. This allows baby to discover how asparagus tastes both raw and cooked, hot and cold.*

From the Kitchen Garden
Vegetables from My Garden
Spring - Summer

**10 months and up**

# Green Asparagus Velouté

[ 20 min

**Useful Utensils**

Cutting board
Paring knife
Mandoline
Chinois
Bowl

**Grocery list for a 1 year old child**

**[ at the market** 1 dozen thin green asparagus spears
1/2 green onion
3 spinach leaves

**[ at the grocery store** 1 tiny pinch salt
1 thin drizzle olive oil
...and a few ice cubes

## Here we go!

[ Stem the spinach leaves. Thoroughly wash the leaves in several rounds of cool water. Set aside. Remove the green onion's outer layer. Cut the onion in half and thinly slice the half to be used. Set aside. Gently wash the asparagus one by one. Cut off the hard, dirty end (3/4 inch) and throw them away. Remove their small "leaves" with a paring knife. Cut the asparagus into thin slices. Place them, along with the green onion, into the steamer basket and cook for 15 minutes (water level 3). Pour the cooking juices into a bowl.

[ Place the cooked asparagus and onions, plus the raw spinach leaves, in the blending bowl.

[ Blend, adding a small amount of cooking juices between each pulse, depending on the desired consistency. Pulse once for a purée with a few asparagus chunks; twice for a more homogenous consistency; or three times for a velouté that will be perfect if you strain it through a Chinois and salt to taste (if necessary).

[ Pour into a bowl and decorate with a thin drizzle of olive oil.

Grandma loves the freshness of this recipe *when we eat it cold on hot summer nights.*

## This recipe's good points:

*This is a sweet, simple, and delicately flavored velouté. The spinach brings out the color and taste in this dish.*

*It's a fresh-tasting recipe that calls for vegetables right out of the garden, from mid-February to the end of June, when asparagus are at their peak.*

*More than just a healthy vegetable, asparagus has been enjoyed since the time of the Egyptians and was a favorite of Louis XIV. It is jam-packed with vitamins and minerals, especially B vitamins and potassium. This little gem has a good amount of soft fibers, which aids intestinal transit, and is a well-known diuretic.*

Mom says:

*When Alphonse was little, I didn't add the raw spinach. And instead of cooking juices, I added some prepared baby formula so that he could drink this velouté from a bottle.*

Chef Dad's Advice:

*To make a Parmentier stew, cook the white part of a new leek (0.75 oz) with the other vegetables and blend with some cooking juices and a pat of butter (but leave out the parsley and milk). To make Vichyssoise, add the fresh parsley to the Parmentier stew recipe before blending. Serve cold.*





6 months and up

# French Mashed Potatoes

All seasons

[ 20 min

**Useful Utensils**

Vegetable peeler
Paring knife
Fork, if necessary

**Grocery list for a 6 month old baby...**

**[ at the market**
1 large Yukon Gold potato
3 sprigs flat-leaf parsley

**[ at the grocery store**
2 Tbsp prepared baby formula
1 small pat butter

**...and for a 1 year old**

1 more Yukon Gold potato
1 Tbsp olive oil (instead of the prepared baby formula and butter)
1 tiny pinch salt (for older babies)

**This recipe's good points:**

*Potatoes are a poorly understood food treasure. They are far richer in carbohydrates than other vegetables, and also full of minerals, trace elements and, surprise, vitamin C! Parsley is a discreet source of calcium and vitamins (K, C, and carotenes). Olive oil is loaded with essential fatty acids. And leeks, the old standard, are full of minerals, carotenes, and soft fiber. They also act as a diuretic.*

## Here we go!

[ **For 6 to 12 month olds:** Rinse the potato, peel it with a vegetable peeler, wash it again, and dice it. Place the pieces in the steamer basket and cook for 15 minutes (water level 3). While the potato is cooking, wash the parsley in water, dry it, and remove the leaves. Throw the cooking juices away. Transfer the potato to the blending bowl and pulse once. Add the parsley leaves, milk, and butter. Pulse once more for a perfect homemade purée.

[ **For babies 1 year and up:** Prepare and cook the potatoes as above, and throw the cooking juices away. Prepare the parsley in the same way and crush the leaves with your hands. Next, smash the potatoes on a plate with a fork. Add the olive oil and parsley. Taste and lightly season, if necessary, and let the young connoisseur be the judge.

Chef Dad's Advice:
*If you add less cooking juices and prepared milk-based pediatric nutritional supplement, you will obtain a cauliflower purée whose consistency you can adapt to your baby's preferences.*



12 months and up

# Cauliflower Curry in a Hurry

[ 20 min

**Useful Utensils**

Large bowl
Paring knife
2 small saucepans
Slotted spoon
Bowl
Tablespoon

**Grocery list for a 1 year old child**

[ **at the market** 1 cauliflower

[ **at the grocery store** 3 or 4 Tbsp prepared milk-based pediatric nutritional supplement (or prepared baby formula for the youngest babies)
1/4 tsp curry (optional)
a few drops white vinegar

## This recipe's good points:

*It's fun to discover cauliflower cooked and (almost) raw. This vegetable deserves to be loved for its concentration in vitamin C and its protective micronutrients, plus its density in soft fiber. Cauliflower is well-loved in France for is gentle, delicate flavor.*

## Here we go!

[ Wash the cauliflower by shaking it off in water. Next, let it soak for a few minutes in the vinegar water. Cut the biggest florets in half, leaving only 1-inch stem. Place 3 or 4 florets in the steamer basket and cook them for 15 minutes (water level 3).

[ While the cauliflower is cooking, boil water in a saucepan. Drop 3 or 4 very small cauliflower florets in the boiling water and leave them to cook "English style" for 30 seconds. Remove them with a slotted spoon. In a second saucepan, heat 3 or 4 tablespoons of milk supplement or formula (the amount depends on the desired consistency of the dish).

[ **When the vegetables have been steamed,** collect the cooking juices in a bowl. Transfer the cooked cauliflower to the blending bowl. Add 1/4 teaspoon of curry. Pulse once. Add 2 tablespoons of cooking juices to the hot milk supplement or formula. Pour it into the blending bowl. Pulse once more.

[ **Pour the cream-colored velouté** into a soup bowl. Place the little blanched florets on top.

[ And let baby sing your praises for this subtly colored dish!

Chef Dad's Advice:

*On summer nights, I make this same gazpacho with pesto for friends, and serve it with breadsticks that I roll in thin slices of smoked ham.*



8 months and up

# Andalusian Gazpacho...

[ 20 min

**Useful Utensils**

Cutting board
Paring knife
Vegetable peeler
Scales
Chinois

**Grocery list for a 1 year old child**

**[ at the market**
1/4 small cucumber
1 large tomato
1/4 white onion
0.35 oz red pepper
3 sprigs basil
1 celery stalk
1 clove new garlic

**[ at the grocery store**
1 tsp tomato paste
1 drizzle Sherry vinegar
and...2 Tbsp crushed ice



## This recipe's good points:

*This recipe is not only fresh and thirst-quenching (full of water), but also extremely nutritional, because cucumbers, tomatoes, and peppers are all good sources of minerals, trace elements, and vitamins (especially C and A). This light recipe with delicious flavors is seasoned by the taste of the celery and the aroma of the Sherry vinegar that was aged for years in oak barrels*

## Here we go!

[ **Remove the leaves from the sprigs of basil.** Rinse the basil leaves, cucumber, tomato, celery, and pepper under running water. Peel the cucumber and cut it into quarters. Remove the tomato stem and the stringy fibers from the celery stalk (from the bottom to the top). Cut the pepper in half, remove the seeds, and cut off the 0.35 oz piece that the recipe calls for. Cut the basil leaves, 1/4 cucumber, tomato, celery stalk, and pepper slice into pieces. Peel the onion. Cut 1/4 of it and the garlic clove into small pieces. Place all of the vegetables (in the amounts specified) into the blending bowl. Add the tomato paste (for color) and crushed ice (for temperature). Blend well (3 pulses) to obtain a homogenous consistency.

[ **If a few chunks still remain after blending,** strain the gazpacho through a Chinois. Add a drizzle of Sherry vinegar to take away any acidity and lightly enhance the gazpacho.

[ **Serve cool,** of course, in a glass or clear bowl, with a tiny dribble of pesto on special days.

For Special Days

# ... with pesto

[ **It's simple, delicious, aromatic, and ready in 5 minutes!** Remove the leaves of 3 sprigs of basil and wash the leaves under running water. Place them in the blending bowl with 0.35 oz of Parmesan Reggiano, 1 tablespoon of pine nuts, and 1 tiny pinch salt (to keep the basil green). Pulse 3 times, adding a little olive oil between each pulse (1/4 cup total) to bind the ingredients to each other.

[ And voilà! And if you want to use it for pasta? Don't change a thing!

Chef Dad's Advice:

*I serve this dish as a first course in the summer when we have guests. I pour the soup into melon-rind bowls placed on beds of ice and sprinkle them with strawberries as well as melon balls.*

8 months and up

From the Kitchen Garden

Mediterranean Fruits and Vegetables

Spring - Summer

# Melon Ball Soup

[ 5 min

**Useful Utensils**

Scissors
Small knife
Teaspoon
Melon baller

**Grocery list for a 1 year old child**

**[ at the market** 1 small, fresh, ripe melon (cantaloupe or Crenshaw)
2 fresh mint leaves

## Here we go!

[ Wash the melon under running water and cut it in half. Remove the seeds with a spoon. Rinse the mint leaves under running water and cut them up with scissors.

[ Take one half of the melon and cut it into two quarters. You will only use one of these quarters. Peel it and cut the flesh into small pieces. Place them in the blending bowl. Pulse twice, adding a small amount (about 1 tablespoon) of slightly mineralized water between the pulses to obtain a light soup. Use the melon baller to scoop little balls from the second half of the melon.

[ Pour the melon soup into half of the rind, add the melon balls, and sprinkle with mint.

[ Serve it "on a platter."

### This recipe's good points:

*This soup refreshes in summer and its slightly sweet taste makes it a great thirst-quencher. Babies love it from the bottle. Mint aids digestion (and helps with headaches, too) and contains a good amount of vitamins (A and B). Melon is great for preventing fatigue. Teeming with vitamins (especially vitamin C), it rivals the kiwi.*

Mom's Advice:

*Without the mint, you can give this melon soup to baby through a bottle starting at 6 months when he or she needs something to drink.*

Chef Dad's Advice::

*Use the rest of the vegetables for the grown-ups: the leftover eggplant in ratatouille… and the extra peppers? For oil-cured peppers!*



**12 months and up**

# Babaganoush

**[ 25 min**

**Useful Utensils**

Scissors
Bowl
Cutting board
Paring knife

**Grocery list for a 1 year old child**

**[ at the market** 1/2 small eggplant
1/4 red pepper
1/4 green pepper
3 or 4 basil leaves

**[ at the grocery store** 1 teaspoon olive oil

## This recipe's good points:

*A Mediterranean taste. The smell of basil. The taste of olive oil (source of vitamin E and essential fatty acids). The sunny colors of the vegetables when bought and while being prepared: the glossy deep purple eggplant, rich in fiber and potassium; and the shiny red and green pepper, rich in vitamins A and C.*

## Here we go!

[ Wash the basil leaves under running water and cut them into fine pieces with scissors. Set aside. Wash the 2 peppers, cut out their stems, remove the seeds, and cut them into quarters. Dice 1/4 of the red pepper and 1/4 of the green pepper. Wash the eggplant, cut off its ends, peel it, and cut it in half. Cut half of the eggplant into pieces. Place the diced pepper and eggplant pieces into the steamer basket and cook for 15 minutes (water level 3). Throw the cooking juices away.

[ Transfer the pepper and eggplant to the blending bowl. Pulse once. Mix with the chopped basil leaves and olive oil.

[ And serve to mama's little helper, who has played with the vegetables and watched their kitchen adventures with a lot of interest!

Mom's Advice:

*You can also serve the avocado mousse guacamole-style, as an appetizer with family or friends, spread on small squares of bread.*

From the Kitchen Garden
Mediterranean Fruits and Vegetables
All seasons

**15 months** for the avocado
**2** or **3 years** for the shrimp



# Avocado Mousse "Our Way"

[ **10 min**

**Useful Utensils**
Cutting board
Paring knife
Scissors
Teaspoon

**Grocery list for a 15 month old child**

[ **at the market** 1/2 avocado
1/2 lemon
2 or 3 basil leaves, or fresh coriander

[ **at the fishmonger's (or the freezer section)**
for toddlers (2-3 years old): 2 or 3 large pink Atlantic shrimp (cooked)

[ **at the grocery store** 1 thin drizzle olive oil

## Here we go!

[ Wash the basil leaves (or fresh coriander) under running water. Cut them up with scissors. Cut the lemon in half with a paring knife. To prevent the avocado from turning brown, do not wash off the knife. Plus, rub the teaspoon with the lemon.

[ Cut the avocado in half with the knife. Use the spoon to remove the avocado flesh from the half that you are going to serve to baby. Keep the avocado skin. Place the flesh in the blending bowl. Add 2 drops of lemon juice (and only 2 drops!), a thin drizzle of olive oil, and the herbs.

[ Pulse twice, if you'd like to pique baby's curiosity by leaving a few avocado chunks in the mousse; or pulse three times for a more homogenous, guacamole-style mousse. Stir with a spatula after each pulse.

[ **For children over 2, you may add pink peeled shrimp** that have been cut into small pieces (by hand or with 1 pulse in the blending bowl).

[ Spoon the mousse into the avocado skin and decorate with a basil or coriander leaf.

Chef Dad's Advice::

*The fresh coriander refines the texture of the avocado. As the child grows, increase the quantity of lemon and decrease the number of pulses so as to combine the chunks of avocado with the shrimp when you add them. Choose extremely fresh shrimp (with shiny, firm shells and a curved tail) or frozen ones.*



## This recipe's good points:

*Eating Avocados introduces baby to a very refined taste; they are an important mixture of essential fatty acids (for the brain, nervous system, and retina) and vitamin E, which helps protect the fatty acids. But wait at least one year so that the digestive system can assimilate this rich fat.*

*Shrimp are a wonderful source of protein and revitalizing mineral salts. But because of the risk of allergies, doctors recommend waiting a little longer, till the age of 2 or 3.*

Grandma says:
*Leave the skin on the baby potatoes because they add a nice taste and are a good source of vitamins.*

From the Kitchen Garden
Seasonal Purées
Spring - Summer

8 months and up

# Purée of Spring Vegetables...

[ 25 min

**Useful Utensils**
Cutting board
Vegetable peeler
Scissors
Paring knife



**Grocery list for an 8 month old baby...**

**[ at the market**
4 fresh peapods
1 small new carrot
1 new turnip
1 green onion
1 small new fennel bulb
1 small purple artichoke
10 market-fresh fava bean pods
2 round baby potatoes
4 sprigs flat-leaf parsley

**[ at the grocery store**
1 thin drizzle olive oil
1 pat butter (if necessary)
a few grains of fleur de sel
1/4 turn of the pepper mill (white pepper)

## Here we go!

[ **Rinse the vegetables in water and then peel each of them,** including the onions. Wash them thoroughly. Leave them whole if they are small. Otherwise, cut them into 2 or 3 pieces. Shell the peas. Shell the fava beans as well, and remove their skin by pinching each bean so it slips out of the skin. Cut the fava beans in 2. Prepare the artichoke last. Cut the stem about 1 inch from the leaves. Peel the remaining stem with a paring knife. Use your hands to remove the biggest leaves from the base of the artichoke. Then cut off the tops of the leaves 1/3 of the way from the top. Place all of the vegetables (except for the parsley) into the steamer basket and cook them for a good 15 minutes (water level 3).

[ **While they are cooking, wash the parsley, cut it up with scissors, and set aside.**

[ **Once everything is cooked,** pour the cooking juices into a bowl. Transfer all of the vegetables to the blending bowl. Pulse at least 3 times for a homogenous purée, adding a small amount of the cooking juices between each pulse.

[ **Spoon the spring purée onto a plate.** Drizzle a small amount of olive oil over it, and sprinkle it with a few grains of fleur de sel and chopped parsley.

...and of Summer Vegetables

[ **To the Purée of Spring Vegetables, add** 1 zucchini and its flower, 2 round red radishes, 2 small green asparagus spears, and 10 very thin French-style green beans.

[ **The zucchini flower is a simple touch** that you can add at the end to make the dish pretty. Remove it from the zucchini and shape it with a knife, for example, into the form of a dragon's crest, to be cut up later.

[ Wash the vegetables under running water and peel them. Snap off the ends of the green beans. Cut of the dirty ends of the asparagus spears and remove their little "leaves". Remove the ends of the zucchini and cut it in half lengthwise.

[ Add these to the vegetables from the Purée of Spring Vegetables. Cook and blend as above, and spoon onto a plate. But finish off the dish with the zucchini flower!

**This recipe's good points:**

*A handful of small new vegetables, tender and fresh, to which summer adds its special touches. Serve these flavorful veggies to smaller babies as a purée, and in colorful little pieces in a mini casserole dish to older babies, and know that your baby, whatever his or her age, is getting a great mix of minerals and vitamins.*

Chef Dad's Advice:

*Starting at 2 or 3 years old, serve the vegetables right from the steamer, without blending them, to emphasize their individual shapes, tastes, and colors. Even better: reduce the cooking juices in a saucepan, add a pat of butter, and pour over the vegetables so that they shine in a clear mini-casserole dish. A summer delight.*

Mom says:
*When I make pumpkin soup, I keep a piece of the pumpkin for the Purée of Fall or Winter Vegetables that I make for Alphonse.*



8 months and up

# Purée of Fall Vegetables...

[ 30 min

**Useful Utensils**
Mixing bowl
Cutting board
Paring knife
Vegetable peeler
Tablespoon
Bowl

**Grocery list for an 8 month old baby**

**[ at the market**
1 small pumpkin slice (1/4 cup of 1″ cubes)
1 leaf Swiss chard
1 small chestnut (frozen!)
1/2 Bosc pear
1/2 Jonathan apple
1 red potato
1 green onion
1/2 lemon

**[ at the grocery store**
1 thin drizzle olive oil
1 pat butter
a few grains of fleur de sel
1/4 turn of the pepper mill (white pepper)

## Here we go!

[ Fill a mixing bowl with lemon water. Wash the Swiss chard and cut the white part away from the green (keep it for another meal). Peel the white part with a vegetable peeler so as to remove all the stringy fibers. Place it in the lemon water in the mixing bowl. Wash the potato and peel it with a vegetable peeler. Remove the pumpkin rind, seeds, and stringy flesh. Remove the green onion's outer layer. Wash the apple and pear, peel them, cut them in half, and remove their cores. Wash the chestnut, score its shell so that it comes off more easily, and cut it in half. Cut the fruits and vegetables into pieces (everything must fit in the steamer basket!). Cook them all for a good 15 minutes (water level 3).

[ Pour the cooking juices into a bowl. Transfer the contents of the steamer basket to the blending bowl. Pulse twice, adding 2 tablespoons of cooking juices between pulses, to obtain a thin purée. Or pulse only once, and add 1 tablespoon of cooking juices, to obtain a more solid purée.

[ Spoon onto a plate. Add a pat of butter and a drizzle of olive oil. Mix, taste, and season with some fleur de sel and a tiny bit of white pepper if necessary.

[ **...and have baby blow on the purée** so that it cools to a temperature that is just right.

Chef Dad's Advice:

*I keep the green part of the Swiss chard to make salmon brandade-style for lunch the next day. I buy tiny, firm fruit: Seckel pears and Jonathan apples. And for Alphonse, I cook his red potatoes with the skin on.*

# ...and of Winter Vegetables

[ **To the Fall Purée, you add** 1 salsify and 5 or 6 grapes (Concord).

[ Carefully rinse the salsify under running water to wash out the dirt. Peel it with a vegetable peeler and cut it into pieces that are 1-1/2 to 2 inches long. Place it in lemon water (along with the Swiss chard) so that it does not brown before cooking it with the rest of the fruits and vegetables.

[ Wash the grapes and leave their skin on. Add them raw to the finished purée of winter vegetables.

### This recipe's good points:

*The tastes of fall from the orchard and the kitchen garden, which you will couple with the tastes of winter. At the market, smell and choose and then cook and eat with the rhythm of the seasons, along with your little one whose eyes, nose, and ears never miss a beat.*

Mom's Advice:

*I substitute smoked reindeer meat from Scandinavia for the bone-in ham.*

From the Kitchen Garden
Winter Market
Winter

**8-10** months and up

# Mom's Little Ham

Chef Dad's Advice:

*Sage goes well with ham, rabbit, and veal. When Alphonse was a bit older, I introduced him to prosciutto instead of bone-in ham, so the dish would have a bit of a stronger taste. He loved it.*

51

### This recipe's good points:

*A love affair between flavors and aromas: the sage brings out the sweetness of the ham, and the ham softens the slight bitterness of the celery root.*

*And a good amount of protein: meat protein and vegetable protein, which gives the body a nice dose of minerals, vitamins, and fiber as well.*

[ 25 min

### Useful Utensils

Cutting board
Paring knife
Vegetable peeler

### Grocery list for a 1 year old child

**[ at the market** 1/4 celery root (2.75 oz)
1 large Yukon Gold potato
1/2 carrot
1 small handful thin French-style green beans
1 small sage leaf

**[ at the butcher's** 1 slice (1.5 oz) bone-in ham

**[ at the grocery store** 1 Tbsp prepared milk-based pediatric nutritional supplement (or prepared baby formula for 8-12 month olds)
1 thin drizzle olive oil
1 tiny pinch salt

## Here we go!

[ Rinse all of the vegetables under running water. Snap off the ends of the green beans. Peel the potato, carrot, and celery root with the vegetable peeler. Wash all of the vegetables and cut them into equal-sized pieces. Place them in the steamer basket and cook for 15 minutes (water level 3). Throw the cooking juices away. Transfer the cooked vegetables to the blending bowl. Add the milk and the sage leaf. Pulse 3 times to obtain a purée.

[ While the vegetables are cooking, remove the fat from the ham and cut it into small pieces.

[ Spoon the purée onto a plate, add a tiny bit of salt (for older babies), and drizzle a bit of olive oil over top. Sprinkle the bits of ham over the purée.

[ Hats off to the chef!

Grandma says:

*This is "Alphonse's dish" when I make endives au gratin for the grown-ups.*

From the Kitchen Garden
Winter Market
Fall - Winter

12 months and up

# Let's Dive into Endives

[ 25 min

**Useful Utensils**
Scissors
Cutting board
Paring knife

**Grocery list for a 1-year-old child**

**[ at the market** 2 endives
1 sprig flat-leaf parsley
A few drops lemon juice

**[ at the grocery store** 2 Tbsp olive oil
1 Tbsp balsamic vinegar
1/4 turn of the pepper mill (white pepper)
1 tiny pinch salt

## Here we go!

[ Start by washing the parsley, removing the leaves, and cutting them up with scissors. Meticulously wash the endives. Remove the bitter white base, as well as any damaged leaves. Keep 6 or 7 nice-looking raw leaves. With a knife, trim the edges so they look like feathers. Cut the endives in half lengthwise. Place them in the steamer basket, sprinkle them with a few drops of lemon juice (to prevent them from turning brown), and cook them for 15 minutes (water level 3).

[ While they are cooking, **make a balsamic vinaigrette** (do not mix it though, to avoid creating bubbles). Add the chopped parsley to it.

[ When the endives are cooked, throw the cooking juices away and transfer the contents of the steamer basket to the blending bowl. Blend as gently as possible (1 pulse). Place this endive "cloud" at the center of the plate and pour the vinaigrette over it. Then place the endive "feathers" around it, just like a daisy.

[ Then watch them pull the petals off the daisy, munch on little feather dipped in vinaigrette, and eat spoonfuls of "clouds."

## This recipe's good points:

A playful way to eat cooked and raw endives. In both preparations, the soft fibers are easily tolerated by the digestive system of a young child. And all this in addition to its richness in water, minerals, trace elements, and folic acid (vitamin B9), which is of the utmost importance for the development of the nervous system.

This often unknown and often unloved vegetable deserves to be appreciated for its important qualities and integrated early on into baby's diet.

Chef Dad's Advice:

*I like this recipe because babies can enjoy the cooked and raw aspects of endives. It is a true discovery of the veggie's natural flavors that does not touch its basic nature.*

Mom's Advice:

*When Alphonse was younger, I replaced the cooking juices in this recipe with prepared milk-based pediatric nutritional supplement, making the velouté sweeter and my little guy's discovery of this vegetable a bit easier.*

From the Kitchen Garden
Winter Market
Winter - Spring

15 months and up

# Fava Bean Velouté...

[ 15 min

**Useful Utensils**

Cutting board
Paring knife
Vegetable peeler
Bowl
Chinois, if necessary

**Grocery list for a 15 month old child**

**[ at the market** 2/3 cups (3.5 oz) fava beans
1/2 baking potato
1/4 green onion
1/2 clove new garlic
1 sprig savory (if necessary)

**[ at the grocery store** 1 Tbsp olive oil

## This recipe's good points:

*Also called broad beans or horse beans, fava beans are the one of the most ancient legumes in cultivation, along with lentils. Prehistoric evidence of their existence has been found. In ancient Rome, a person who found one in his or her dish was "crowned" king or queen of the banquet, which is where the French "galette des rois," or King's cake, tradition comes from.*

*This tiny treasure is a good source of energy, is rich in carbohydrates, fiber, and protein, and is tender and easily digestible when cooked, making it extremely good for baby.*

## Here we go!

[ Shell the fava beans and remove their skin by pinching each bean so it slips out. Cut them in half. Rinse the potato under running water, peel it with the vegetable peeler, and wash it. Dice the half that you are going to use. Remove the green onion's outer layer. Thinly slice one quarter of it. Cut the garlic clove in half. Place the vegetables, in the quantities outlined above, into the steamer basket. Cook for 10 minutes (water level 2).

[ Pour the cooking juices into a bowl. Transfer the steamer basket's contents to the blending bowl.

[ Pulse twice for a purée and three times for a velouté, adding enough of the cooking juices between each pulse to obtain the desired consistency.

[ **You can remove large pieces** by straining the velouté through a fine strainer or a Chinois. Then serve your smooth purée or velouté with a thin spiral of olive oil drizzled on top.

# ...and Fava Bean Purée

[ **This goes deliciously well with lamb and certain types of fish,** like hake, sea bass, turbot, and even red mullet. Chef Dad follows the same directions as for the fava bean velouté, except that he only adds a bit of the cooking juices while blending so as to obtain the consistency of a true purée. And before cooking the fava beans in the steamer basket, he adds a sprig of savory.

Grandma says:

*This way, when I prepare salt pork with lentils for my family, I also have a recipe for the "little guy," so no one is jealous!*

From the Kitchen Garden

Winter Market

Winter

3 years and up

# Lentil and Dry-cured Ham Velouté



[ 5 min the night before + 20 mn

**Useful Utensils**

Mixing bowl
Strainer
Saucepan
Cutting board
Paring knife
Vegetable peeler
Parchment paper
Nonstick pan
Paper towel
Bowl

**Grocery list for a 3 year old child**

**[ at the market** 1/3 cup green lentils
1/2 celery stalk
1/2 carrot
1 sprig thyme

**[ at the butcher's** 1 slice dry-cured ham (0.35 oz)

**[ at the grocery store** 1 slice sandwich bread
1 drizzle grapeseed oil
1 Tbsp thick crème fraîche
1 tiny pinch salt

Chef Dad's Advice:

*To make croutons, take a slice of sandwich bread, remove the crust with a knife, and cut the center into small cubes. Toast them with a drizzle of grapeseed oil in a frying pan until golden brown (not dark brown though!). Soak up some of the oil by letting them cool on a paper towel.*

**This recipe's good points:**

*The richness of lentils! These vegetables have the second-highest amount of protein, right behind soybeans, and are richer in carbohydrates than whole grains. They are also dense in fiber, and easily digestible because they lack cellulose. They contain seven times more iron than spinach...etc. So there are many good reasons why they have been a staple food since ancient times, from the Middle East to the Mediterranean basin. Plus, the marriage of thyme and dry-cured ham brings out a wonderful taste.*

## Here we go!

[ **The night before,** prepare the lentils. Wash them thoroughly by picking them over on the palm of your hand to eliminate any possible stones. Leave them to soak overnight in a mixing bowl full of water so that they expand and become softer.

[ **The following day,** drain the lentils using a strainer. Place them in a saucepan of cold water. "Blanch" them on the stove until they boil. Drain them again. Cut the celery stalk in half lengthwise. Wash the half that you are going to use and cut it into small pieces. Wash half of the carrot, peel it, and cut it into pieces. Rinse the thyme under running water.

[ Line the bottom of the steamer basket with 2 layers of parchment paper. Pour in the lentils. Add the carrot, celery, thyme, and dry-cured ham in the quantities outlined above. Cook everything for 15 minutes (water level 3). Pour the cooking juices into a separate bowl. Transfer the vegetables to the blending bowl. Pulse three times, adding some cooking juices between each pulse to obtain a nice-looking velouté. Don't skimp on the cooking juices, because this velouté tends to be rather thick.

[ Pour the velouté into a soup bowl. Spoon a dollop of crème fraîche onto the middle. Sprinkle the croutons around it, if you've decided to make it a bit more sophisticated for your young connoisseur.

[ **Serve right away,** while the crème slowly melts...



*Sometimes I add a little piece of dry-cured ham. This adds a "rustic" flavor to the recipe and brings out the taste. Alphonse loves it!*

Chef Dad's Advice:
*Successfully making socca depends entirely on how it is cooked. The cake must be crunchy on the outside and soft on the inside.*

From the Kitchen Garden
Winter Market
All seasons

3 years and up

# Rosemary Chickpea Purée...

[ **5 min the night before + 20 min**

**Useful Utensils**
2 bowls
Strainer
Cutting board
Paring knife
Whisk

**Grocery list for a 3 year old child**

[ **at the grocery store** 1/2 cup (2.75 oz) dry chickpeas
1 Tbsp olive oil

[ **at the market** 1/4 green onion (if possible)
1 small sprig rosemary

## This recipe's good points:

*Chickpeas have many good qualities. They are nutritious, full of calories, and an excellent source of folic acid (vitamin B9), a substance important in the development of a child's nervous system. They supply the body with a large amount of protein, carbohydrates, and fiber. But the digestive system does not tolerate this vegetable until the age of 2 or 3.*

*Rosemary, a Mediterranean herb, brings out the chickpea's subtlety.*

*This little legume helps children to explore international flavors because it is an ambassador of Middle Eastern cooking (couscous, hummus, and falafel). Socca, a traditional French cake made with chick pea flour, is originally from Turkey and was introduced to France by way of Italy.*



## Here we go!

[ The night before, soak the chickpeas in a large bowl of water to allow them to expand and soften during the night. The following day, drain the chickpeas in a strainer and rinse them thoroughly under running water. Remove the green onion's outer layer and thinly slice one quarter of it. Rinse the rosemary and pull its needle-like leaves off the stem.

[ Place the chickpeas, onion, and rosemary leaves in the steamer basket. Cook them for 15 minutes (water level 3). Pour the cooking juices into a bowl.

[ Transfer the contents of the steamer basket to the blending bowl. Pulse 2 or 3 times, adding a bit of cooking juice and a very small amount of olive oil between each pulse to obtain a homogenous consistency.

[ **And what does our little taste tester say?** As a rule, he or she should savor this slowly...

...and, For Special Days:

# ... Socca Niçoise

[ **Try it: it's simple to make, and oh, so good!** Preheat the oven to 425 °F (gas 7). Heat 1/2 cup of water in a small saucepan. When it starts to simmer, sprinkle 1/2 cup (about 1.5 oz) of chickpea flour into the saucepan and beat it vigorously to obtain a dough. Cook for 3 or 4 minutes. When it becomes unstuck from the saucepan, place it in the blending bowl with a drizzle of olive oil and blend to rid the dough of all lumps (3 pulses). Spread it out in a pie pan and place it in the oven for 5 minutes.

**Eggs, dairy products, cheese, poultry, and ham: the farm is... a hen that lays golden eggs of animal proteins! When these ingredients meet certain quality criteria, standards that are so important for a child's health, they offer a little something extra.**

**The egg is an ingredient of immense qualities,** an almost perfect food (except for a lack of carbohydrates). The yolk has the upper hand over the white in terms of calcium, phosphorus, iron, iodine, vitamins A, D, E, and B9, fat, and calories. To have the best taste and quality, buy eggs from "free-range chickens" or organic farms. Buy them "farm-fresh," with their packaging date clearly marked on the box. "Farm-fresh" eggs are ones that were laid less than 7 days ago. They are considered "fresh" from day 7 to 21. Keep the eggs away from strong-smelling ingredients, because their shells are porous.

**Dairy products are also loaded with protein and calcium, a unique pair of qualities that only milk can furnish. Fromage blanc** (Italian ricotta included) is neck and neck with **curd cheese** ("grandma's curdled milk") and yogurt (fermented milk). Easily digestible and light, they are a good way, starting at 12 months, to meet baby's daily milk requirement: at least half a liter every day to grow big and strong, with healthy bones and sharp teeth.

**Cheeses are even more nourishing:** they are dense in everything, especially fat and calories. They also contain minerals, with Parmesan and Gruyere being the richest in calcium and phosphorus. And let's not forget trace elements (iron) and vitamins (A, D, B2, and B12). Cheese stimulates digestion and encourages intestinal flora, whether it is hard cheese (Gruyere and Parmesan), soft cheese (Camembert), or goat cheese. Choose "farmhouse, "artisanal," and "AOC" cheese and you'll get even more applause (starting at 1 year).

**Butter (raw) is extremely valuable** for its vitamin content (A, D, and E). Serve a small pat at 4-6 months, and a bigger pat later on.

**And let's not forget crème fraîche, the lightest of the fats,** with its vitamin A and calcium!

**Poultry has the same nutritional value as meat, but is leaner - that's its advantage.** It has the same protein, iron, potassium, and vitamin content, and is even richer in phosphorus. That's why chicken and turkey breast are recommended for babies starting at 5-6 months—but skinless, of course! Buy them from the butcher, ideally. Ask for top quality items, such as free-range chicken and heritage turkey. Choose a bird with thin skin and firm flesh, which is white or yellowish, depending on if it was raised on wheat or corn.

**Ham contains just as much protein, iron, and potassium as poultry, but more fat,** carbohydrates, and calories. Baby can eat this starting at 5-6 months, provided that it is boiled, lean (or extra lean), and high-quality: bone-in ham, for example (cooked in a bouillon).

# Down on the Farm

Chef Dad's Advice:

*This recipe is pleasing to the eye, and to the stomach when served cold.*

Down on the farm
Eggs and Cheeses
Spring - Summer

12 months and up

# Egg-cellent Caponata

[ 25 min

**Useful Utensils**

Cutting board
Paring knife
Vegetable peeler
Scissors
Saucepan
Slotted spoon

**Grocery list for a 1 year old child**

**[ at the market** 1/2 eggplant
1 small plum tomato
1 green onion
1/2 sweet pepper
1 clove new garlic
a few basil leaves and sprigs flat-leaf parsley
3 large pinches pine nuts
1 "farm-fresh" free-range egg

**[ at the butcher's** 1 slice lean boiled ham, sliced thinly like prosciutto

**[ at the grocery store** 1 thin drizzle olive oil
1 tiny pinch salt



**This recipe's good points:**

*This dish's taste is very subtle...and is a complete, balanced meal. The fiber and potassium in the eggplant; the calcium and vitamin K in the parsley; vitamins A and C found in large sweet peppers (twice as much is found in the red bell peppers); the protein in pine nuts, the fruit of the pine tree with a sophisticated and enjoyable taste, and excellent brain food; the protein and vitamin B1 in boiled ham (lean, and nice and pink!). Plus the egg, which is an almost perfect food.*

Grandma says:

*With the playfulness of the vegetable's colors and shapes, this dish is fun to make. Let your little one enjoy the process, too. Place him beside you. Slip a long sleeved bib on him and a big apron on yourself. When he sees the surprise that you are preparing, he will be even more excited to "discover" the result.*



## Here we go!

[ Wash the vegetables under running water (rinse them several times) before preparing them. Cut the stem out of the pepper, cut the pepper into quarters, and remove the white membranes and seeds. Dice the 2 quarters to be used. Cut the tomato into four pieces, peel it, and dice it. Peel the eggplant with a vegetable peeler, cut it in half, and cut the half you are going to use into 3 or 4 slices. Remove the green onion's outer layer. Thinly slice the green onion and garlic clove, but use just enough of each to season the caponata when your child is of a tender age. Place the desired quantities in the steamer basket and cook for 15 minutes (water level 3).

[ While the vegetables are cooking, wash the herbs under running water and cut them up finely using scissors (except for one basil leaf, which you should keep for garnish).

[ **To cook the poached egg,** boil salted water in a saucepan. Break the egg into the saucepan, wait 5 minutes, and remove it with a slotted spoon. Place the egg on top of the thinly sliced ham. Fold the ham around the egg like a little present.

[ The vegetables are cooked. Throw the cooking juices away. Transfer the vegetables to the blending bowl along with the herbs, 3 pinches of pine nuts, and a thin drizzle of olive oil. Pulse once to obtain a "caviar-like" consistency with a few chunks, or twice for a frothy consistency. Taste and add a bit of salt, if necessary.

[ **Spoon the caponata onto the plate next to the ham-egg "present,"** and decorate it with the basil leaf to add a bit of color.

[ The surprise is all ready!

Chef Dad's Advice:

*When shopping at a Mediterranean market, choose smaller zucchinis. I use fat-free fromage blanc because it stays together better.*



Down on the farm
Eggs and Cheeses
Spring - Summer

12 months and up

# Zucchini Flan-tastic

[ 25 min

**Useful Utensils**

Cutting board
Pastry brush
Paring knife
Teaspoon
Whisk
Small mixing bowl
Ramekin
Small gratin dish

**Grocery list for a 1 year old child**

[ **at the market** 1 zucchini (around 5.25 oz)

[ **at the cheese shop** 1 "farm-fresh" free-range egg
2 Tbsp fat-free fromage blanc
1 small pat butter

## Here we go!

[ Before doing anything else, preheat the oven to 300 °F (gas 3).

[ **Butter the ramekin** (just like chefs do: from the bottom to the top with a pastry brush, so that the flan rises easily), and place it in the refrigerator for around 10 minutes to cool, long enough to make the recipe.

[ Wash the zucchini thoroughly under running water because you will leave the skin on to add a little color to the dish. Cut into quarters lengthwise. If it contains too many seeds, remove them with a spoon. Place the pieces in the steamer basket and cook for 5 minutes (water level 1). Throw the cooking juices away. Transfer the zucchini to the blending bowl. Blend to obtain a homogenous consistency (2 or 3 pulses). Let cool.

[ While the vegetables are cooking, beat the egg in a mixing bowl to the egg. Add the fromage blanc, a small pat of butter, and the cooled zucchini. Fill the ramekin half full with this mixture. Reduce the oven temperature to 250 °F (gas 2). Pour a little bit of water in the gratin dish. Place the ramekin in it. Place the double boiler in the oven for 15 to 20 minutes.

[ **Check that the flan is done** by inserting a knife in the center. If the blade pulls out clean, the flan is ready for the taking.

Mom says:

*In fact, this is "Alphonse's special recipe" for zucchini flan that the whole family loves.*

**This recipe's good points:**

A light and complete meal, easily digestible and refreshing, this flan melts on the tongue and is sweet to the palate. The calcium found in fromage blanc teams up perfectly with the phosphorus found in eggs and makes for healthy bones and beautiful teeth. The density of minerals and the mix of vitamins found in zucchini will get baby into shape.

12 months and up

# Spinach Purée

[ 10 min

**Useful Utensils**
Cutting board
Paring knife

**Grocery list for a 1 year old child**

[ **at the market** 7 cups (7 oz) fresh spinach

[ **at the grocery store** 1 Tbsp heavy cream
and…for older children: 1 tiny pinch salt

**This recipe's good points:**

*Spinach is the healthiest fresh vegetable, with its copious amounts of mineral salts and vitamins, on top of its well-known richness in fiber, and its high iron content, famous since the days of Popeye. It is not recommended for children under 12 months because of its potentially high nitrate content (if it is not from a kitchen garden or an organic farm). Choose young plants with fresh, tender, shiny, deep green leaves. But don't let it trick you: raw spinach cooks down a lot.*

## Here we go!

[ Stem the spinach leaves and wash them in a colander under running water. Place them in the steamer basket and cook them for 5 minutes (water level 1). Throw the cooking juices away.

[ Transfer the spinach to the blending bowl. Add approximately 1 tablespoon of slightly mineralized water and pulse once. Add the cream and pulse a second time.

[ The resulting mixture will be a creamy purée. Serve as is (add a little salt, if necessary) or with a soft-boiled, fried, or scrambled egg.

# On special days, with Ricotta Gnocchi...

[ Cut 1 cup (9 oz) of ricotta (goat or sheep's milk) into pieces. Place it in the blending bowl with 1/4 cup of flour, 1 teaspoon of olive oil, and 1 pinch of grated nutmeg. Break the egg into the blending bowl. Pulse 3 times.

[ Heat a saucepan of water. Form the dough into olive-sized balls using a teaspoon dipped in hot water. Poach the gnocchi in simmering water until they rise to the surface (30-40 seconds).

[ Serve warm on top of the spinach purée with a drop of olive oil and a pinch of fleur de sel.

# ... or Spinach-Mozzarella Tagliatelli Nests

[ Cook 3.5 oz of tagliatelli (fresh, if possible) and carefully combine it in a mixing bowl with the spinach purée. Add 1 diced mozzarella di Bufala Campana. Watch the cheese melt slowly. Turn the pasta with a fork to form little spinach-tagliatelli nests.

Chef Dad's Advice:

*To change things up and introduce baby to the joys of raw and cooked together, set aside some tiny spinach leaves. Use them to decorate the tagliatelli nests.*

Down on the farm
Eggs and Cheeses
All seasons

12 months and up

# Curd Cheese and Herbs

Grandma says:
*I started by giving baby the plain curd cheese, and then added a drizzle of olive oil and a different type of herb (and only one type) each time I made the dish, so as to figure out which flavors my grandson preferred (or hated!).*

[ 5 min

**Useful Utensils**
Dish towel
Scissors
Teaspoon
Tablespoon
Ramekin

**Grocery list for a 1 year old child**

[ **at the cheese shop** 2 rounded Tbsp curd cheese (1 oz) or fresh curdled milk

[ **at the market** 1 sprig chives
1 sprig chervil
1 sprig tarragon
1/4 shallot

[ **at the grocery store** 1 thin drizzle walnut oil
and...stale bread for toasting (or crostinis)

### This recipe's good points:

*A daring recipe because it introduces baby to a whole new world of fine herbs and seasonings. But sensible because it brings together a bouquet of healthy ingredients and tastes that a baby of strong character will appreciate. In fact, it is the child's version of "cervelle de canut," a traditional cheese dish that silk workers in Lyon ate in the 19th century.*

## Here we go!

[ Rinse the herbs under running water, shake them off to remove any dirt, dry them in a dishtowel, and cut them into coarse pieces with scissors. Peel the shallot and chop it finely. Place 1 teaspoon of chives, 1 teaspoon of chervil, 1/2 teaspoon of tarragon, and 1/2 teaspoon of shallot into the blending bowl. Blend just a little (1 pulse) so as not to reduce it to a pulp. Add the curd cheese, stir, and blend again (1 pulse). Pour the flavored curdled milk mixture into the ramekin. Toast the bread in a toaster or under the broiler. Serve it alongside the curd cheese.

[ **Right before serving, drizzle a bit of walnut oil over top.** And let baby dip the bread right in, but not his fingers!

Grandma says:

*A child should already be able to chew quite well to keep the walnut crumbs (even very tiny ones) from going down the "wrong tube."*

Down on the farm
Eggs and Cheeses
All seasons

3 years and up

# Curd Cheese and Herbs

[ 5 min

**Useful Utensils**

2 tablespoons
Small bowl

**Grocery list for a 3 year old child**

[ **at the market** 3 whole walnuts or 6 shelled walnuts (dried)

[ **at the cheese shop** 1/4 cup low-fat fromage blanc
1 pinch salt

[ **at the grocery store** 1 Tbsp Acacia honey
or 1/4 tsp cinnamon powder

## Here we go!

[ Crack open the 3 walnuts and remove the 6 walnut halves.

[ Place 5 of the halves in the blending bowl. Pulse twice to chop them into "crumbs."

[ Add the fromage blanc. Pulse once more.

[ **Spoon into a small bowl,** drizzle the honey over it, and serve.



Chef Dad's Advice:

*I choose Acacia honey because it is a delicacy and has a light taste. Sometimes I substitute it with cinnamon powder (1/4 teaspoon). I start preparing this recipe the day before by soaking the walnut halves in milk for a few hours to bring out their taste.*

**This recipe's good points:**

*This recipe helps to make little guys strong because the animal proteins found in the fromage blanc (in addition to the calcium and iron) team up with the vegetable protein found in nuts (and their essential fatty acids). Plus, walnuts are even more dense in calories when dried than when fresh.*

Grandma says:

*This recipe's subtitle could be "how to eat leeks and not know it!"*

Down on the farm
Eggs and Cheeses
Spring - Summer

6-8 months and up

# Free-Range Chicken Breast with Broccoli

[ 30 min

**Useful Utensils**

Mixing bowl
Saucepan
Cutting board
Paring knife
Vegetable peeler
Plate
Plastic wrap

**Grocery list for a 1 year old child**

**[ at the butcher's** 1 free-range chicken breast (about 3 oz)

**[ at the market** 3 small broccoli florets
3 small red potatoes
1/2 small plum tomato
1/2 white part of a thin pencil leek

**[ at the grocery store** 1 pinch salt
1 thin drizzle olive oil
1/4 turn of the pepper mill (white pepper)
a few grains fleur de sel

**This recipe's good points:**

*This is a healthy meal for delicate palates. The sweet taste of the red potato (full of energy) balances out the bitterness of the leek (soft fibers and diuretic action), as well as the acidity of the tomato (dripping with vitamins and minerals). And the broccoli adds a good dose of beta carotene (promotes growth and good vision) and especially vitamin C (boosts the body's immune system) to the mix.*

Chef Dad's Advice:

*I recommend free-range chicken, because it guarantees that the animal was carefully raised, and red potatoes, for the sweet taste they bring to the dish and which makes them the preferred spud of children.*

## Here we go!

[ Pour cool water into a mixing bowl. Bring a saucepan of water to a boil.

[ **To prepare the chicken breast,** remove its skin, cut the flesh into small pieces, and place it directly into the steamer basket. Cook for 10 minutes (water level 2).

[ **While the chicken is cooking, prepare the vegetables.** Cut 3 broccoli florets with a 1-inch stem. Remove the roots from the leek. Cut the top part of the leek into quarters lengthwise. Wash the vegetables under running water and shake them with the top facing down to get rid of any dirt. Cut the white part of the leek in half lengthwise and chop 1/2 of the white part into thin slices. Remove the tomato stem. Cut the tomato in half (you will only use half). Rinse the potatoes in water, peel them with a vegetable peeler, and wash them before dicing them.

[ When the diced chicken is cooked, throw the cooking juices away, and transfer the meat to a plate. Cover it with plastic wrap to keep it warm.

[ Place the broccoli florets, half of the white part of the leek, half of the tomato, and the potato into the steamer basket. Cook them for 15 minutes (water level 3). Throw away the cooking juices. Transfer the vegetables to the blending bowl (with the diced chicken for little ones) and pulse twice to obtain a purée.

[ Spoon the vegetable purée into a soup bowl. For older babies, sprinkle the diced chicken over top. Drizzle with a small amount of olive oil.

[ **For the biggest kids,** lightly season and liven up the dish with a few grains of fleur de sel.

[ And what does the little boss think?

Chef Dad's Advice:

*Almost all children love pumpkins because they are soft, slightly sweet, and melt in your mouth. Let's make the most of this by adding ham to the menu for the first time.*

Down on the farm

Eggs and Cheeses

Fall - Winter

8 months and up

# Ham and Pumpkin Au Gratin

73

## This recipe's good points:

*Sweet tastes, harmonious colors, playful consistencies... The ham-pumpkin combination is particularly good at seducing wary little ones into trying new things, and at nourishing their little bodies with the minerals found in pumpkin (extremely rich in potassium) and the protein found in high-quality boiled ham, which is just as good as the protein found in red meat.*

[ 30 mn

### Useful Utensils

Cutting board
Paring knife
Cheese grater
Bowl
Tablespoon
Ramekin

### Grocery list for a 1 year old child

[ **at the market** 5.25 oz prepared pumpkin (= 1 medium-sized slice)

[ **at the butcher's** 3 oz boiled ham, thick slices (1/4 inch thick)

[ **at the cheese shop** 0.75 oz fresh Parmesan
1 generous-sized pat butter

[ **at the grocery store** 3 good-sized Tbsp prepared milk-based pediatric nutritional supplement... (or prepared baby formula for 8 to 12-month-old babies)
1 tiny pinch salt
1/4 turn of the pepper mill (white pepper)

## Here we go!

[ **Start by cutting the fat off the ham.** Cut the ham into tiny pieces (watch your fingers!), grate the Parmesan (1 tablespoon), and set both of them aside.

[ **Next, prepare the pumpkin.** Wash it, remove the rind and seeds, cut the flesh into pieces, and place them directly in the steamer basket with a tiny pinch of salt. Cook for 15 minutes (water level 3).

[ Preheat the broiler.

[ Pour the cooking juices into a bowl. Place the cooked pumpkin in the blending bowl with the milk and butter. Pulse 3 times to obtain a smooth, liquid consistency. If necessary, add a small amount of cooking juices (1 tablespoon at most) between 2 pulses. Transfer to the mixing bowl. Add the ham pieces, a bit of salt, and a tiny bit of pepper. Mix well and pour into the ramekin. Sprinkle with the grated Parmesan.

[ **Bake** for 10 minutes for a sunny-colored gratin (10 min).

Mom's Advice:

*When I have a busy schedule, I prepare the pumpkin purée the day before. It only takes a few minutes to heat up.*

Grandma says:

*At Christmas, I cut a piece of white meat from the traditional turkey and serve it to Alphonse with two holiday purées: chestnut and celery.*

Down on the farm
Eggs and Cheeses
Winter

18 months and up

# Tom, Tom the Turkey

[ 20 min

**Useful Utensils**
Cutting board
Small knife

**Grocery list for an 18 month old child**

**[ at the market** 1 small Savoy cabbage

**[ at the butcher's** 1.75 oz turkey breast
1 small slice country smoked bacon (0.75 oz)

**[ at the grocery store** 1 small pat butter
1 tiny pinch salt
1/4 turn of the pepper mill (white pepper)



## Here we go!

[ Prepare the cabbage by removing its first layer of leaves, which pull away easily, as well as the core. Cut the cabbage into quarters. Wash them in a large bowl of water that has a teaspoon of vinegar in it.

[ You will only use 1/4 of the cabbage for this recipe (keep the rest for a "grown-up" meal!). Cut the leaves into strips that are not too thin and place them in the steamer basket.

[ Thinly slice the turkey meat and bacon. Add them to the steamer basket with the butter.

[ Cook everything for 15 minutes (water level 3). Throw the cooking juices away.

[ Lightly season with salt (not too much because the bacon is already salty!) and pepper. Taste and add more, if necessary.

[ Spoon onto your little angel's plate and serve as is.

Chef Dad's Advice:

*Choose a Savoy cabbage, with curly leaves and a firm heart, and preferably a heritage turkey. And the little tiny piece of country-smoked bacon is added to give the dish a little something extra.*



**This recipe's good points:**

When baby discovers the pieces of turkey hidden in the tender cabbage leaves, it helps him to develop a taste for two different flavors and two consistencies. Plus, baby will get his fill of vitamin C (to strengthen your body's defenses, little one) and protein in a hearty winter meal.

**To nourish a child is to build something new...a little guy or girl who will grow up to feel comfortable with him or herself. Meat, with its first-class proteins and its iron, which the body assimilates easily, is the best type of building block after milk. Chef Dad uses it with panache on Special Days in recipes from Scandinavia (Pytt-i-Panna) and the Middle East (Moroccan Kefta). And demands only the highest quality items with each purchase. It is true that this quality is expensive, but there is no use brooding: happiness comes from the countryside!**

**It doesn't matter whether you choose red or white meat, because they have the same nutritional value.** Both are roughly equivalent to boiled ham and poultry... with the exception of their fat content. Choose tender cuts of lean meat: minute steak and skirt steak; lamb shoulder, neck, and leg; and veal loin...from a good butcher.

**A good butcher respects the meat he sells. He chooses only the best:** regional, artisanal, farm-fresh, high-quality ingredients that have been carefully chosen from farms that raise their animals the natural way, in green pastures and wide-open fields. Their meats are well-preserved and well-prepared. A good butcher gives advice and grinds meat upon request before your very eyes, and knows that the little morsels are intended for little mouths. He'll recommend that you place your purchases directly in the fridge and eat them within 3 hours—cooked Chef Dad-style, of course, whether as meatballs or veal cakes.

**Buy organic red meat from farms such as Niman Ranch in California.** It should be red, shiny, and firm. And if you buy frozen ground beef, make sure it is "5% fat" (extra lean) and that it goes right from the freezer to the Babycook!



**You can find pink lamb meat all year round, or the cream of the crop, milk-fed lamb meat** from December to April. Make sure to buy it with its regional label.

**And for white meat? Milk-fed veal calves** from an organic farm.

**But make sure to restrict baby to mini-portions: 1 teaspoon at around 5-6 months,** following your pediatrician's advice. Increase to 1 tablespoon at around 12 months, and 2 tablespoons at 2 years old (1-1.75 oz). Always serve it at lunch, so that at night baby will sleep, well, like a baby.

**That doesn't seem like a lot! But, actually, it is. Babies often eat too much meat too soon...** Twice a week is plenty, if you alternate it with eggs, ham, poultry, and fish, which are all good sources of the animal protein that will eventually replace the protein in mother's milk or formula completely.

**What do animal proteins do?** They furnish all of the body's elements, and feed and protect the body. Iron helps to oxygenate red blood cells. Meat also contains: **copper,** which helps the liver to use iron; zinc, which is necessary for growth; **potassium,** which is important for a balanced nervous system; and **B vitamins,** which feed the cells with energy.

**And busy bodies must be fed day after day... but not too much!**

77

# In the Pasture

Mom says:

*Make sure to slip a long sleeved bib onto baby. You won't regret it...*

In the pasture

Meats

All seasons

12 months and up

# Mary Had a Little Lamb (Kefta)

[ 20 min

**Useful Utensils**

Cutting board
Paring knife
Small mixing bowl
Plastic wrap
Vegetable peeler
Small saucepan
Wooden spoon
Teaspoon

**Grocery list for a 1 year old child**

[ **at the butcher's** 3 oz lamb (shoulder, neck or leg)

[ **at the market** 1 sprig fresh coriander
1/4 Spanish onion
...and for the sauce: 1 medium-sized baking potato

[ **at the grocery store** 1/2 tsp cumin powder
olive oil
...and for the sauce: 1 tsp tomato paste

## Here we go!

[ Wash the fresh coriander under running water and remove the leaves. Peel the onion and cut it into quarters. Dice 1/4 of the onion. Cut the lamb into large pieces and place them directly in the blending bowl. Add the olive oil, diced onion, fresh coriander leaves, and cumin. Pulse 3 times to obtain a smooth mixture. Transfer the mixture to a mixing bowl, cover with plastic wrap, and let rest in the refrigerator.

[ **While the mixture is resting, prepare the sauce.** Rinse the potato, peel it with a vegetable peeler, wash it, and dice it. Heat the olive oil in a saucepan over low heat. Add the diced potato and sweat it for 30 seconds without allowing it to brown. Add just enough water to cover the potatoes. Add the tomato paste and allow it to thicken while stirring gently. The sauce will turn an appetizing red color. Remove from heat.

[ **Now it's time to make the lamb meatballs.** Remove the meat mixture from the refrigerator. Roll it with the palms of your hands into 5 or 6 meatballs the size of a cherry. The chef's little assistant will be watching you! Drop the meatballs in the sauce and cook them for 6 or 7 minutes over low heat. Serve this mouth-watering meatball ragout when it is nice and red. Who will be able to resist picking out the little meatballs with their fingers?

**This recipe's good points:**

*In this deep red sauce, baby will discover a new spice: cumin. Its warm taste will bring out the lamb's tenderness and flavor. This dish will stimulate his eyes and taste buds, as well as his curiosity and imagination.*



Chef Dad's Advice:

*With meatball recipes, I play the game "journey around my plate" with Alphonse. I have him taste both the Moroccan Kefta meatballs and Swedish Kött Bullar meatballs (pronounced "schott boullar").*

Chef Dad said:
*In fact, this is the baby version of "grown-up couscous" (without harissa and merguez sausage. That way everyone can join in the fun.*

In the pasture

12 months and up

Meats

Fall - Winter

# My First Couscous

**This recipe's good points:**

*This recipe wins the prize for most balanced meal: animal protein from the meat, vegetable protein from the vegetables (along with the complete array of essential amino acids), and carbohydrates from the couscous semolina (a favorite starting at 6 months). This dish from the sunny country of Morocco is a meal in and of itself.*



Mom's Advice:
*Discovering food from other cultures early on opens the palate and new horizons. And that's a good thing.*

[ 25 min

**Useful Utensils**

Soup bowl
Plastic wrap
Cutting board
Paring knife
Fork
Mixing bowl
Teaspoon

**Grocery list for a 1 year old child**

**[ at the grocery store** 3 Tbsp (1 oz) medium-grain couscous semolina
1 tsp olive oil
1 pat butter

**[ at the market** 0.75 oz carrot
0.75 oz thin French-style green beans
0.75 oz zucchini
0.75 oz turnip
0.75 oz celery root
1 sprig fresh coriander
2 mint leaves

**[ at the butcher's** 0.75 oz ground lamb (shoulder, neck, or leg)
0.75 oz ground free-range chicken breast

81

## Here we go!

[ **Prepare the couscous semolina.** Place the couscous semolina in a soup bowl. Add enough hot water to cover the couscous grains, cover the bowl with plastic wrap, and allow it to expand while you are preparing the rest of the recipe.

[ Wash all the vegetables as well as the sprig of fresh coriander (but not the mint). Peel the carrot, zucchini, turnip, and celery root, and snap the ends off the green beans. Cut them into large pieces and place them in the steamer basket. Cook for 10 minutes (water level 2). Throw the cooking juices away. Add the ground meat, add water up to level 1, and cook for 5 more minutes.

[ While it is cooking, rip the 2 mint leaves into pieces. Use a fork to transfer the couscous semolina to a mixing bowl and break up the clumps. Add the butter, olive oil, and mint. Gently mix and set aside.

[ **The meat and vegetables are cooked.** Throw the cooking juices away. Transfer the cooked food to the blending bowl. Pulse once so that some pieces remain. If the pieces are too large for your child to chew, pulse once more. Spoon the couscous semolina onto your little angel's plate, make a little well in the middle, and pour the sauce into the middle. Bon appétit!

Chef Dad's Advice:

*Make sure the meat mixture spends enough time in the fridge! If the meat is cool, the meatballs will be easier to roll and won't fall apart in the frying pan.*

In the pasture

Meats

Fall - Winter

15 months and up

# Swedish Meatballs

[ 25 min

**Useful Utensils**

Small knife
Cutting board
Bowl
Fork
Plastic wrap
Vegetable peeler
2 small mixing bowls
Nonstick pan
2 soup spoons

**Grocery list for a 15 month old child**

**[ at the butcher's** 1.5 oz minute steak
1.5 oz lean pork belly

**[ at the cheese shop** 1 "farm-fresh" free-range egg
1 Tbsp thick crème fraîche
2 small pats butter

**[ at the market** 1 large new potato
1/4 Spanish onion

**[ at the grocery store** 2 Tbsp prepared milk-based pediatric nutritional supplement
1 tiny pinch salt
1/4 turn of the pepper mill (white pepper)

**This recipe's good points:**

*"Kött Bullar"( pronounced "schott boullar"!), or Swedish Meatballs, is a recipe made on the weekend in Sweden. This delicious dish is a treat for kids in the fall and warms them in winter. And it's not surprising, with its many health benefits: the meatballs are loaded with protein (beef and pork, which are also good sources of iron), stuffed with vitamins (dairy), and full of calories (carbohydrates in the potatoes). And an egg, the perfect food, to boot.*

## Here we go!

[ **To prepare the meat mixture,** place the pieces of meat in the blending bowl. Pulse twice. Peel the onion, thinly slice 1/4 of it, and add it with the milk to the meat mixture. It's the egg's turn now…but only add half of it! Break the egg into a bowl, beat it with a fork, and pour half of it into the blending bowl. Season very lightly.

[ **Pulse once to obtain a homogenous mixture** (or twice, stirring between pulses). Transfer to a mixing bowl, cover with plastic wrap, and let sit for 10 to 15 minutes (at least) in the refrigerator.

[ While the meat is resting, wash the blending bowl, and prepare the side dish. Rinse the potato under running water, peel it with a vegetable peeler, wash it, and cut it into small pieces. Place it in the steamer basket. Cook for 10 minutes (water level 2). Throw the cooking juices away. Transfer the potato to a mixing bowl, smash it with a fork, and add the crème fraîche and a small of pat butter. Mix. Keep in a warm place.

[ Remove the meat mixture from the refrigerator and roll it between the palms of your hands into 4 or 5 meatballs the size of a chestnut.

[ **Melt a small pat a butter in a frying pan.** As soon as it starts to bubble, place the meatballs in the pan and brown them on all sides, cooking them for 5 minutes in total.

[ Place the meatballs on the plate. Form the mashed potatoes into 2 dumplings with 2 soup spoons. Add them to the plate as a yummy decoration. What will our little food lover dive into first?

Mom's Advice:

*This recipe is for the days when I really pull out all the stops.*
*In order to save some time, I ask my butcher to cut the meat into small pieces with a knife right in front of me.*

*The raw beet surprised Grandma. She wanted to make sure it was good… and she admits that it is.*

In the pasture

Meats

Fall - Winter

12 months and up

# Pytt-i-Panna

[ 15 min

**Useful Utensils**

Cutting board
Vegetable peeler
Small knife
Bowl

**Grocery list for a 1 year old child**

[ **at the butcher's** 3 oz beef cut into large cubes
1 slice smoked h am (0.75 oz)

[ **at the market** 2 small Yukon Gold potatoes
1/4 onion
1/2 carrot
... and 1/4 raw beet

[ **at the grocery store** 1 Tbsp heavy cream

## Here we go!

[ Let's start with the raw beet. Wash, peel, and dice it.

[ Next, rinse the other vegetables under running water, peel them, and wash them. Cut the desired quantities into small pieces. Place everything in the steamer basket. Add the cubes of meat and smoked ham. Cook everything for 10 minutes (water level 2). Throw the cooking juices away.

[ Transfer the cooked ingredients to the blending bowl. Pulse once to blend slightly (some small pieces should remain). Empty into a mixing bowl and add the cream.

[ Spoon the mixture onto a plate. Sprinkle the raw beet cubes on top.

[ And now the Swedish Hash is ready to win over another fan…

Chef Dad's Advice:

*When buying the beef, choose a topside beef cut into large cubes with a knife so that the pieces don't fall through the holes in the steamer basket.*



### This recipe's good points:

*In Sweden, Pytt-i-Panna is THE "dish for little boys." They love it because everything is cut into tiny bits. And as big people often are nostalgic for their childhood, it has become a recipe in its own right. This is true for Mi, Alphonse's mom, who is Swedish*

*Protein from the beef, carbohydrates and fiber from the vegetables, calories from the small amount of smoked ham, and vitamin A from the cream. This recipe is definitely one that will chase away the winter blues!*

Mom says:

*To introduce Alphonse to a plethora of condiments, I place little dishes full of different sauces around his plate, where he can dip his veal cakes as he pleases.*

In the pasture

12 months and up

Meats

Fall - Winter

# Veal Cakes...

[ 30 min

**Useful Utensils**

Dish towel
Scissors
Cutting board
Knife
Small mixing bowl
Plastic wrap
3 bowls
Fork
Nonstick pan

**Grocery list for a 1 year old child**

**[ at the butcher's** 1 oz veal loin

**[ at the market** 2 sprigs flat-leaf parsley

**[ at the cheese shop** 1 tsp heavy cream
2 "farm-fresh" free-range chicken eggs
1 small pat butter

**[ at the grocery store** 1 rounded Tbsp flour
3 Tbsp breadcrumbs
1 Tbsp grapeseed oil
1 tiny pinch salt
1/4 turn of the pepper mill (white pepper)

## This recipe's good points:

*A "crunchy" way to prepare veal. It has been ages since baby was introduced to this tender, lean meat. But this recipe presents it in a more elaborate form, with a different consistency. A step toward becoming a connoisseur of fine fare...*

*The mushroom purée that goes with it so well is made with button mushrooms, or "champignons de Paris», as they are called in French. Although they arrived in France rather recently (even though they were around in Ancient Egypt), this variety of mushroom quickly became the most cultivated in the world! And rightly so, for it is rich in minerals, trace elements, and vitamins, and has a soft texture that is pleasing to the tongue.*

## Here we go!

[ **Let's start by preparing the meat mixture.** Wash the parsley under running water and shake it well. Remove the leaves from the stem and dry them in a dish towel. Cut the leaves up with scissors. Dice the veal and place it in the blending bowl along with the parsley and heavy cream. Add the egg as well. Pulse 3 times, stirring between each pulse with a spatula to obtain a fine, dense mixture. Season lightly. Transfer the mixture to a mixing bowl, cover with plastic wrap, and let rest in the refrigerator for 15 to 20 minutes.

[ While the mixture is resting, line 3 bowls up in a row. Place the flour in the first bowl. Break an egg in the second and beat it. Place the breadcrumbs in the third.

[ **When the meat mixture is cool, form it into little "pucks"** (flattened meatballs) with the palms of your hands. Pick up each puck with a fork and dip it in the flour, then in the egg, and finally in the breadcrumbs, tapping it each time on the edge of the bowl to remove any excess ingredient. Set the pucks aside. Heat a small pat of butter and a tablespoon of grapeseed oil in a frying pan over medium heat. When it starts to bubble, reduce the heat, and brown the pucks on both sides.

[ And the veal cakes are ready to crunched on by little chompers!

Chef Dad's Advice:

*It is ideal to use veal from milk-fed calves that were not weaned from their mother's milk. And why should the mixture spend some time in the refrigerator? Because that way the cakes are easier to make and don't fall apart while cooking.*



On Special Days:

# ...and Button Mushroom Purée

## Here we go!

[ Clean 3.5 oz of button mushrooms (5.5 medium sized mushrooms) in lemon water. Wash 1 small Yukon Gold potato and dice it. Place them in the steamer basket with a splash of lemon juice and cook for 10 minutes (water level 2). Throw the cooking juices away*. Pulse 3 times, adding 1 tablespoon of heavy cream between each pulse, plus a tiny pinch of salt, if necessary.

* Unless you would like to thin the purée down to a velouté!

**Iodine, phosphorus, and protein direct from the sea, with fluoride and potassium in their wake. Fish, shrimp, and scallops: a pirate's treasure that delights nutritionists and makes Chef Dad wriggle with inspiration.**

**Fish is one of the best foods around...when it is fresh as a daisy, with** shiny eyes, red gills, glistening scales, and a healthy smell. Otherwise, sail on and buy it frozen, because frozen fish are processed on the boats they are caught on and are extremely fresh—but their flesh will be drier.

**Serve lean fish to your little first mate,** like sea bass, cod (the leanest fish and one of the most rich in potassium), plaice, dab, whiting, and sole (serve it cooked through; the flesh should be a pearly white)...and pike, a favorite fresh water fish.

**Warning: fragile!** Ask the fishmonger to bone it (but we'll keep our eyes out for little bones that he might have missed). You can your purchase for a short amount of time in the refrigerator, wrapped in aluminum foil so that their sea smell won't permeate other food. Then, carefully cook them right away. Start by giving baby small amounts at around 5-6 months and watch for any signs of allergies. And if everything goes well, fish will be on the menu 2 or 3 times a week!

**Try salmon out on your budding seafood-lover at around 12 months: this cold water fish is exceptionally rich in essential fatty acids and vitamins A and D—** which goes hand in hand with a fish's fat content. But make sure to choose wild salmon from Norway or Scotland that is less than 3 years old, the only types that still follow their ancestors' migration ritual.



**As for scallops, be as patient as a fisherman's wife and wait for at least 18 months before serving baby this treat,** until the risk of allergies to their high iodine content disappears. That doesn't mean, however, that you shouldn't still start with small mouthfuls to be sure.

**Iodine,** which is only present in seafood, is necessary for growth... but don't overdo it! **Selenium** strengthens the immune system. **Fluoride** gives baby teeth the strength to take a bite out of life. **Phosphorus** makes for strong bones, beautiful teeth, and healthy growth, when calcium is also available, and with a little help from vitamin D. The **vitamin D** in fish fat helps the body to assimilate calcium and phosphorus, whereas **essential fatty acids** hold the key to brain development.

**You can never eat too much seafood to grow up as happy as a...clam.** Here are a few recipes that play on their different forms: petals, tartare, brandade, and dumplings, with fennel, Swiss chard, broccoli, spinach, and button mushrooms.

**Now it's time for mom to let her imagination run wild: the range of possibilities is as wide as the ocean!**

89

# High Tide

Mom says:

*If you can't find Atlantic sea bass, regular sea bass is a good substitute.*

High Tide

Fish

Winter - Spring

8 months and up

# Sea Bass with Dill...

[ 20 min

**Useful Utensils**

Cutting board
Paring knife
2 mixing bowls
Small saucepan
Wooden spoon

**Grocery list for a 1 year old child**

**[ at the fishmonger's** 1 oz wild Atlantic sea bass

**[ at the market** 1/4 fennel bulb
1 small dried fennel stalk
1/2 small plum tomato
2 basil leaves
3 drops lemon juice

**[ at the grocery store** 1 drizzle olive oil
1 tiny pinch salt
...and a few ice cubes

## Here we go!

[ Wash the fennel bulb under running water and cut it into quarters. Cut one of the quarters into thin slices. Cut the sea bass filet into thin strips. Place the sea bass and sliced fennel into the steamer basket. Cook for 15 minutes (water level 3).

[ While they are cooking, **prepare a tomato vinaigrette to go with the fish.** Fill a mixing bowl with water and ice cubes. Boil a saucepan of water. Wash the tomato and stem it. Dip it into the boiling water for 30 seconds and then into the ice water before peeling it. The skin should come off very easily. Wash the basil, remove the leaves from the stems, and rip the leaves into pieces. Cut the tomato into quarters, remove the seeds (it's easy to do with your thumb), and cut 2 of the quarters into small pieces. Mix the chopped tomato in a mixing bowl with the olive oil, salt, basil, and 3 drops of lemon juice (and no more!). Set aside.

[ Once the sea bass is cooked, throw the dried fennel stalk and cooking juices away. Transfer the sea bass and cooked fennel to the blending bowl. Pulse twice. Spoon the mixture onto a plate, and sprinkle with the tomato vinaigrette.

[ Isn't it lovely?

91

Chef Dad's Advice:

*Choose wild Atlantic sea bass over its farmed cousin. The latter can be found more easily, but the flesh is much less tender because it has never swum in the sea!*

## This recipe's good points:

*The subtle flavors will sharpen the taste buds. The delicate taste of the sea bass is brought out by the fennel, which is a "sweet dill" with an aniseed-like taste. Used dried and fresh (its winter and spring forms), fennel is rich in sodium and calcium.*

Chef Dad's Advice:

*Ask the fishmonger to cut you a nice-looking cod filet that will stay firm during preparation and have him remove the bones*

High Tide

Fish

Spring - Summer

8 months and up

# Cod Petals and Broccoli Buds

[ 15 min

**Useful Utensils**

Cutting board
Small knife
2 plates
Plastic wrap
Mixing bowl
Scissors
Fork

**Grocery list for a 1 year old child**

**[ at the fishmonger's** 1 small piece fresh cod (1.5 oz)

**[ at the market** 1 small bunch fresh dill
3 or 4 broccoli florets
1/2 lemon

**[ at the grocery store** 1 pinch salt (for older children)

## Here we go!

[ Shake the head of broccoli off in cool water. Cut off 3 or 4 florets. Place them in the steamer basket and cook for 5 minutes (water level 1). Throw the cooking juices away. Smash the florets on a plate with a fork. Cover with plastic wrap to keep them warm.

[ Cut the dill up with scissors. Sprinkle it over the cod (don't skimp!) and place the cod in the steamer basket. Cook for exactly 3 minutes (water level 0.5) so that the fish remains firm. Throw the cooking juices away.

[ Slide the cooked cod onto a plate. Use the tips of your fingers to separate the "petals," or flakes, from one another.

[ Baby is really interested in all of this! Layer the cod petals and the broccoli buds on baby's plate, just like a green and white mille-feuille... and dig in!

### This recipe's good points:

A healthy dish. This light and easily digestible recipe is suitable for one of baby's first «real meals." Quick to make, even if it does take a certain touch to make the mille-feuille look just right. Brings together two ingredients that are great for the body: a lean fish and a beneficial vegetable that baby can enjoy starting at 4 months of age.

High Tide

Fish

Spring - Summer

12 months and up

# Salmon Brandade with Swiss Chard

### This recipe's good points:

*The prince and the pauper finally meet! Unites a "cold water fish," famous for its essential fatty acids, and a vegetable straight from our gardens whose qualities are not always recognized. Together, they are a gold mine of valuable minerals and the vitamins the body needs to assimilate them.*

[ 20 min

**Useful Utensils**
Small gratin dish
Cutting board
Paring knife
Vegetable peeler
Saucepan
Slotted spoon
Mixing bowl
Fork

**Grocery list for a 1 year old child**

**[ at the fishmonger's** 3 oz wild salmon filet

**[ at the market** 1 large Yukon Gold potato
2 leaves French Swiss Chard
1 sprig thyme
1 garlic clove

**[ at the grocery store** 2 Tbsp prepared milk-based pediatric nutritional supplement
1 Tbsp breadcrumbs
1 small pat butter
1 tiny pinch salt

## Here we go!

[ Preheat the broiler. Butter the gratin dish. Bring a saucepan of salted water to a boil.

[ **Prepare the vegetables:** separate the green part of the Swiss chard leaves from the white (which we won't use in this recipe). Wash the green part under running water and cut it into strips (not too thin). Rinse the potato in water, peel it, wash it, and dice it. Place the vegetables in the steamer basket and cook for 10 minutes (water level 2).

[ While they are cooking, prepare the salmon. Pour the milk into a saucepan and add the thyme and unpeeled garlic clove. Warm over low heat. When the milk starts to simmer, add the salmon, and turn off the heat. Poach the salmon for no more than 5 minutes so that it remains tender. Remove the salmon with a slotted spoon. Place it in a mixing bowl, break it up with a fork, and set it aside.

[ When the vegetables are cooked, throw the cooking juices away, and transfer the vegetables to the blending bowl. Pulse 3 times.

[ **Mix the salmon with the vegetables.** Season to taste with a tiny bit of salt, if necessary. Transfer the mixture to the gratin dish. Sprinkle some breadcrumbs over top and brown under the broiler for 5 minutes.

Chef Dad's Advice:

*With this dish, your baby will finally "break bread!" You can substitute cod for salmon, thus making the dish one step closer to a true brandade. And don't forget to use the white part of the Swiss chard for a grown-up gratin.*

Chef Dad's Advice:
*Buy a very fresh small sole from your fishmonger and have him bone it.*

High Tide

Fish

Spring

12 months and up

# Heart and Sole

[ 20 min

**Useful Utensils**

Cutting board
Plastic wrap
Paring knife
Mixing bowl
Saucepan
Slotted spoon
2 toothpicks

**Grocery list for a 1 year old child**

**[ at the fishmonger's** 2 filets sole

**[ at the market** 5 cups (5 oz) fresh spinach
1/2 lemon

**[ at the grocery store** 1 pinch salt
2 pats butter
...and a few ice cubes

## Here we go!

[ Flatten the sole filets (without smashing them!) by covering them with a sheet of plastic wrap, lightly moistening it, and pressing them down with the flat edge of a knife. Fill a mixing bowl with cool water and ice cubes. Place a saucepan of salted water on to boil.

[ Stem the spinach leaves by hand. Wash them thoroughly, changing the water several times. Blanch them for 30 seconds in boiling water and then plunge them in the ice water (to preserve their bright green color). Remove them with a slotted spoon and squeeze them with your hands to remove any excess water.

[ Sprinkle the sole filets with salt and butter them with a knife. Place a layer of spinach on top of each filet, then roll the filets. Pierce them with a toothpick to hold the rolls together. Place both rolls in the steamer basket and cook for 7 to 8 minutes (water level slightly above 1). When they are cooked, cut them in slices.

[ **And voila! Beautiful multi-colored spirals,** almost ready to go down the hatch! Place the half lemon on the edge of the plate to squeeze a few drops of lemon on each slice.

And watch baby trace
the green spiral of spinach
between the layers
of sole with his finger.

### This recipe's good points:

Magic on your plate... this balanced dish combines essential fatty acids from a lean white fish with all the rich minerals of a green, leafy vegetable. Fresh sole is tender (it is drier when bought frozen) and spinach melts in your mouth. A playful combination to help little ones accept this veggie that is often pushed away...

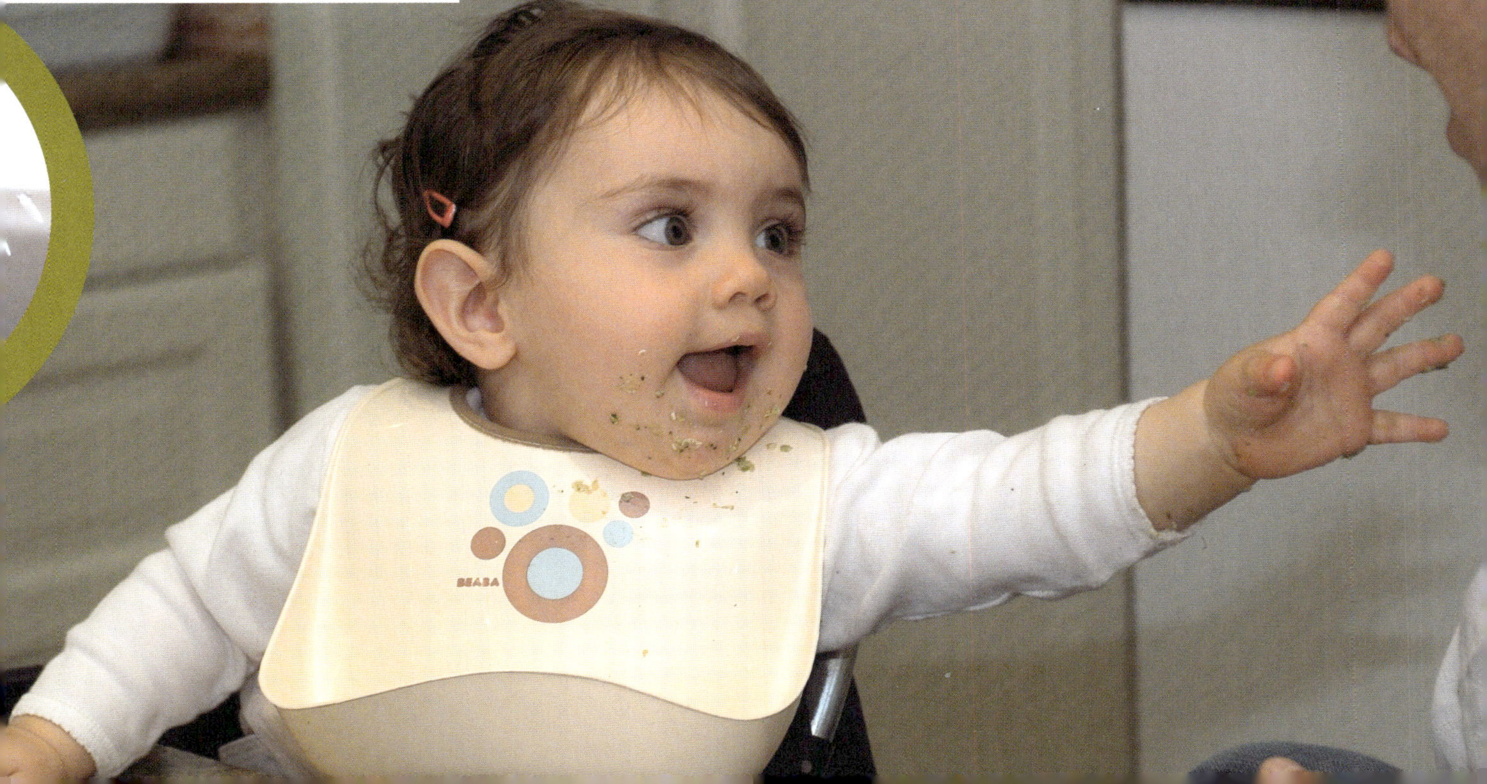

Chef Dad's Advice:
*Choose whichever fish you like, as long as it is white, thin, and extremely fresh. Ask your fishmonger to bone it.*



# Fish Dumplings in Mushroom Sauce

12 months and up

High Tide
Fish
All seasons

[ 15 min for the dumplings [ 10 min for the sauce

**Useful Utensils**
2 small mixing bowls
Plastic wrap
Cutting board
2 small saucepans
Bowl
2 spoons (size of spoons depends on the size of dumplings desired)
Slotted spoon

**Grocery list for a 1 year old child**

**For the dumplings...**

**[ at the fishmonger's** 2 oz white meat fish: whiting, hake, sole, or pike

**[ at the cheese shop** 2 Tbsp butter
1 "farm-fresh" free-range egg
1 Tbsp heavy cream

**[ at the grocery store** 1 tiny pinch salt
1/4 turn of the pepper mill (white pepper)

**...and for the sauce**

**[ at the market** 2 oz button mushrooms (3.5 medium sized mushrooms)
1 shallot
1 sprig thyme

**[ at the cheese shop** 2 Tbsp heavy cream
1 pat butter

**[ at the grocery store** 1 tiny pinch salt
1/4 turn of the pepper mill (white pepper)

Mom's Advice:

*To save time, I make the fish mixture and the sauce the night before. (I take the butter out of the fridge beforehand so that it is soft). All I have to do then is reheat the sauce and cook the dumplings right before suppertime!*

**This recipe's good points:**

*An introduction to a professional chef's recipe, with the freedom for artists to let their creativity flow when making the dumplings (into the shape of a little white mouse, for example!). And the assurance that baby is getting all the virtues the sea has to offer, even if he or she does not like fish...dumplings melt in your mouth, and who doesn't like that!*

## Here we go!

[ **Prepare the fish mixture first.**
Place the fish you have chosen into the blending bowl to chop it finely (1 pulse). Add the butter to the blending bowl. Break the egg into it. Pulse again. Add the cream, a bit of salt, and a very little bit of pepper. Pulse once more. Taste to see if there is enough salt (for baby) and add more, if necessary. Transfer the mixture to a mixing bowl, cover with plastic wrap, and place it in the refrigerator. Wash the blending bowl.

[ **While the mixture is resting, make the mushroom sauce.**
To prepare the mushrooms, remove the dirty end of their stems, wash them twice in a big bowl of cool water, and cut them in half. Peel the shallot and chop it finely. Warm a pat of butter in a saucepan over low heat. Sweat the shallot and mushrooms in it for 30 seconds without browning them. Add the cream, the thyme, and a little salt. Cook for 5 minutes. Remove the sprig of thyme. Transfer the contents of the saucepan to the blending bowl and pulse 3 times. Salt to taste (depending on the child's preferences). Set aside.

[ **Now make the dumplings.**
While the sauce is cooking, heat a saucepan of salted water without allowing it to boil. Remove the fish mixture from the refrigerator. Use 2 spoons (that you've dipped in the hot water so the mixture won't stick to them) to form large or small dumplings, depending on the spoons you have chosen. Use the slotted spoon to place them in the hot water to cook. Cook them for 2 minutes (for large dumplings) and then remove them with the slotted spoon. Place the dumplings in the young connoisseur's soup bowl and cover them with the mushroom sauce.

[ Shhhhh! We're eating!

High Tide
Seafood and Shellfish
Winter

18 months and up

# Scallop Tartare

[ 10 min

**Useful Utensils**
Pastry brush
Paring knife
Cutting board
Mixing bowl

**Grocery list for an 18 month old child**

**[ at the fishmonger's** 2 nice-looking scallops (and their shells)

**[ at the market** 1 blade chives
1 shallot

**[ at the grocery store** 1 or 2 tiny, crunchy cornichons (French pickles)
1/2 teaspoon capers
1 thin drizzle olive oil
1 tiny pinch salt
1/4 turn of the pepper mill (white pepper)

## Here we go!

[ Carefully clean the scallops with a pastry brush under a trickle of water. Then wash the shells under running water. Cut the cornichons into large pieces. Thinly slice the shallot (you'll only use a pinch). Place the cornichons, shallot, and capers in the blending bowl. Pulse once. Chop the chives with a knife and set aside.

[ Next, cut the scallops into small pieces and place them directly into the blending bowl. Pulse twice, stirring between the pulses to redistribute the pieces. Add the chives and the cornichon/caper/shallot mixture. Pulse once more. Transfer the mixture to a mixing bowl. Lightly season to taste (just a little!). Add a thin drizzle of olive oil. Mix.

[ Spoon little piles of the scallop tartare onto the center of the shells and introduce your little one to the magic of the sea…



Mom's Advice:

*Scallops can be difficult to remove from their shells. I ask my fishmonger to do it for me and wrap the scallops and shells up separately.*

Chef Dad's Advice:
*Frozen scallops are not good for tartares. Make sure to choose only the freshest scallops (alive, with a tightly closed shell, and odorless). Handle them as little as possible before preparing the recipe because they should be eaten raw.*



## This recipe's good points:

*Scallops are extremely healthy when eaten in season, from the end of September to March. Their flavor and firm flesh will hook children right away and make them seafood fans for life. But wait for the right age. Their iodine content can provoke allergic reactions in little ones, so wait until your child is at least 18 months old before testing this delicacy out... using a sailor's caution.*

**Harvesting from near and far: in addition to all the seasonal fruits in our markets, we also can enjoy a variety of tropical fruits all year long... You can always have your own favorites, even when you're no bigger than a peanut. But as long as I've been a mother, I've never seen a child turn his nose up at fruit completely... which is a good thing.**

**Fruits are a wonderful source of water, vitamins, and fiber:** vitamin C, which is so important for stimulating the body, metabolism, and immune system, and found in berries and citrus fruit, and especially in kiwis and black currants; carotenes for beautiful skin, found in orange fruits (oranges, apricots, mangos, etc.); fiber (pectin among others), which quickly influences intestinal transit, causing moms to wisely watch their baby's intake of summer fruits. Just because it's good for you doesn't mean we should overdo it.

**We can find all of those qualities in veggies, too... but they're not sweet!**

**The sweet taste of fruit is what baby likes most when he starts tasting them (cooked) at around 4 months,** for fruit with soft fiber (otherwise, wait until baby is at least 15 months), but not until at least 6 months – and with care even then – when there are allergy risks (strawberries).

**On the other hand, fruits contain very few carbohydrates, with the exception of** chestnuts and bananas. They also contain no protein.



**And only nuts contain fat,** which makes up for their lack of water (almonds, walnuts, hazelnuts, pine nuts, etc.)

**Fruit from the orchard, the woods, and berry bushes should be picked or bought ripe.** Especially apricots, which don't ripen after picking, unlike pears. So, buy fruit ripe, but not overripe. It should be sweet-smelling enough to attract bees to its tree, bush, or espalier.

**Tropical fruit should be bought with a recipe already in mind.** Bananas should be yellow and spotted. Pineapples should be fresh and fragrant, with a proud plume and an "air shipped" label. Mangoes should be soft and either green or yellow. Kiwis should be bought firm and slowly ripened in a basket next to an apple.

**Fruits are fragile. Handle them with care** to avoid leaving finger bruises. Keep them for a few days (not more, please!) at room temperature and not in the refrigerator if they contain water (and most of them are full of it). Wash them before peeling and cut them into pieces before cooking and blending them. Baby should eat cooked fruit for a while and, when older, can eat them cooked when having digestive problems.

**Refreshing, thirst-quenching, stimulating, and often purifying, fresh fruits are almost always tolerated (and liked) in soups, compotes, and marmalades.** The best? Quince (only eaten cooked) is a valuable antidote when bigger kids, who can reach fruit baskets, have eaten too much.

# 103 Harvest Baskets

Chef Dad's Advice:

*You can serve this quince compote as a dessert and the cooking juices as a snack, served in a glass or a baby bottle, with a piece of gingerbread for older children.*

Harvest Baskets

Fruit from the Orchard

Fall

6 months and up

# Quince Compote

[ **20** min

**Useful Utensils**

Cutting board
Paring knife
Bowl

**Grocery list for a 1 year old child**

[ **at the market** 1 slightly ripe quince
a few drops of lemon juice

[ **at the grocery store** 1 tsp sugar

**This recipe's good points:**

*Because of richness in soft fibers, quince is as valuable as rice and carrots for intestinal troubles. Plus, connoisseurs enjoy it more because it's only used in sweet dishes... like this one.*

## Here we go!

[ Wash the quince, peel it, cut it into quarters, and remove the core and seeds. Sprinkle some lemon juice on the quarters to prevent them from turning brown. Dice the flesh.

[ Place the quince, sugar, and 2 or 3 drops of lemon juice into the steamer basket. Cook for 15 minutes (water level 3). Pour the cooking juices into a bowl. Transfer the diced quince to the blending bowl. Pulse 3 times, adding a bit of the cooking juice between each pulse to obtain a smooth compote.

[ And what do we think?

Grandma says:

*I substitute an apple for the peach and use the apple compote to make apple turnovers.*

Harvest Baskets

Fruit from the Orchard

Spring - Summer

**6** months and up

# Peach-Vanilla Compote

[ **25** min

**Useful Utensils**

Small knife
Bowl
Piece of fabric (linen, burlap, cheesecloth)
Kitchen twine

**Grocery list for a 1 year old child**

[ **at the market** 2 perfectly ripe yellow peaches

[ **at the grocery store** 1 Tahitian vanilla bean
2 Sarawak black peppercorns
2.5 Tbsp superfine sugar

## This recipe's good points:

*A cool recipe for warm weather, made with cooked fruit that is easy on the digestive system, and a team of exotic flavors that brings out the peach's wonderful flavor: Mexican or Tahitian Vanilla, and the more daring (but worth trying) Malaysian pepper, which adds a subtle touch that is often appreciated by future connoisseurs.*

## Here we go!

[ Take a small piece of fabric, place the peppercorns in it, and tie it up with a piece of kitchen twine.

[ Wash the peaches under running water and peel them (to easily remove the skin, experts run the back of a knife over the entire surface of the peach first). Cut the peach into quarters, pit it, and place the pieces in the steamer basket. Place the vanilla bean and pepper sachet on top of the peach in the basket. Cook for 15 minutes (water level 3).

[ When the peach is cooked, remove the vanilla bean and pepper sachet, and pour the cooking juices into a bowl. Split open the vanilla bean and scrape the seeds out with a knife. Transfer the cooked peaches to the blending bowl, sprinkle with the sugar and a touch of vanilla, and pulse once. Taste to make sure there is enough vanilla flavor, and add a bit more vanilla if necessary. Make sure that the compote is the right consistency for your baby's age and, if necessary, add a bit more of the cooking juices and pulse once more to obtain a smooth compote.

[ **Serve either lukewarm or cold.**

Chef Dad's Advice:

*Go easy on the vanilla. It should compliment the peach, but not overpower it. Also, you can try this recipe with fruits other than peaches. Pears are a good option, for example.*

**8** months and up

# Cherry Granité

[ **10** min, then **30** min in the freezer

**Useful Utensils**

Cherry pitter
Paring knife
Small saucepan
Wooden spoon
Fork
Small bowl (approximately 4 inches)

**Grocery list for a 1 year old child**

[ **at the market** 7 oz dark sweet cherries
2 or 3 drops of lemon juice

[ **at the grocery store** 1/2 cup (3.33 oz) slightly mineralized water
1 Tbsp superfine sugar

## Here we go!

[ Wash the cherries under running water. Stem them and pit them with a cherry pitter (or by cutting them open with a knife). Place them in the blending bowl. Pulse just once to blend and to keep small pieces of fruit, too.

[ Pour the water and sugar into a saucepan. Cook over low heat until the mixture boils. Remove from the heat, add the sugar syrup and 2 or 3 drops of lemon juice to the blended cherries, and mix.

[ Pour the mixture into a bowl and place it in the freezer. Leave it there for at least 30 minutes. Remove it and scrape the "frozen fruit" with a fork to obtain small chips of granité ice.

**This recipe's good points:**

*A light and easily digestible recipe that is cool, sweet, and restorative, too, because cherries are revitalizing. As easy to make as it is to eat...but be careful, because cherry juice can stain!*

Chef Dad's Advice:

*As a surprise dessert for older babies, scoop this granité on top of a cherry clafoutis, for an unexpected and playful "raw on cooked" dessert. They'll love it.*

Mom's Advice:

*Two fresh snacks that are pretty and wonderfully hydrating during the dog days of summer (especially the watermelon, which is extremely rich in water…as its name would have you believe!)*

# ...and Watermelon Granité

## Here we go!

[ During the summer, switch things up with a Watermelon Granité. Use 1 slice of watermelon. Cut the fruit from its rind and remove the seeds. Cut it into pieces. Pulse once and mix with the syrup. Freeze, scrape, and enjoy!

*Alphonse loves mango hedgehogs, and likes to peck at their "prickles" and savor the marmalade while scrunching his little eyes up with pleasure.*

Harvest Baskets
Tropical Fruit
All seasons

**6** months and up

# Mango Hedgehog and Marmalade

[ **15** min

**Useful Utensils**

Paper towel
Cutting board
Paring knife

**Grocery list for a 1 year old child**

[ **at the market** 1 mango, preferably from South-East Asia

[ **at the grocery store** some sugar, if desired

## Here we go!

[ Wipe off the mango before cutting it in half lengthwise. Remove the pit.

[ Each half will be used differently. The first half will become the hedgehog, with a few slices of a knife and a flick of the thumb. Use the knife to cut the flesh in a checkerboard pattern, cutting deeply enough to reach the skin. Do not cut the fruit away from the skin! Use your thumbs to push the fruit inside-out and watch the hedgehog spring to life.

[ Use the other half to make the marmalade. Peel it and dice the flesh. Place it in the steamer basket and cook for 10 minutes (water level 2). Throw the cooking juices away. Transfer the fruit to the blending bowl. Blend lightly (1 pulse) so as to keep some small, tender chunks. Taste and sprinkle with a bit of sugar, if necessary.

[ Place the hedgehog at the center of baby's dessert plate and spoon the marmalade around it. And just watch his reaction!



Chef Dad's Advice:

*Why yellow mangoes from South-East Asia? Because they are the most flavorful, and flavor and consistency are of the essence of this recipe for 2 desserts. Twice the fun!*

## This recipe's good points:

*Fun to look at, easy to make, delicious to eat, easy to digest, and good for the body (fit as a fiddle with provitamin A). Good for body and soul!*

Mom's Advice:

*For a crunchy little addition, I sprinkle crumbled cookies (such as ginger snaps) between each layer. Swedish ginger snaps, or "Pepparkakor" (pronounced "pepacoca"), are Alphonse's favorites!*

Harvest Baskets
Tropical Fruit
All seasons

**8** months and up

# Tropical Treat

[ **15** min

**Useful Utensils**

Cutting board
Paring knife
Teaspoon
Small, clear bowl

**Grocery list for a 1 year old child**

**[ at the market**
1/2 kiwi
1/2 passion fruit
1/4 small Golden Ripe pineapple
1/4 papaya
1/4 Alphonso mango (if possible)

**This recipe's good points:**

*This recipe is refreshing, appetizing, and pleasing to the eye... if the instructions are carefully followed in order. It is also a cocktail of vitamins (especially vitamin C), sugar, and soft fibers if prepared with extremely ripe fruit (except for the pineapple, which should be bought the day of, and the kiwi, which should be bought when firm and allowed to ripen at home).*

## Here we go!

[ Wash all the fruit under running water before peeling them with a knife.

[ Cut the kiwi and passion fruit in half. Cut the mango, pineapple, and papaya into quarters lengthwise. Pit the mango and remove the core from the pineapple. Remove the papaya seeds with a spoon. Set aside the fruit not being used for this recipe (for a tropical fruit salad for older children or grow-ups, perhaps).

[ Next, assemble this colorful dish by blending the fruit separately and spooning it in layers into a small, clear bowl. Start with the half kiwi. Dice it and place it in the blending bowl. Pulse once. Remove the mixture with a spatula and place it in a small, clear bowl.

[ Repeat these instructions with 1/4 of the mango, 1/4 of the pineapple, 1/4 of the papaya, and 1/4 of the passion fruit.

[ And admire your hard work, both of you!

Chef Dad's Advice:

*A fresh, tropical dessert that will warm your eyes and heart like nothing else on cold winter days! I prefer Alphonso mangoes because they are the best in India… what a coincidence that my little guy is named Alphonse!*

**It's been ages since we have sent little ones to bed without their dessert. And rightly so, because desserts balance out the menu and are made with love...which is the icing on the cake!**

**The flavor should be a delight... but a subtle delight,** thanks to the fructose found in a nicely ripe piece of fruit or a touch of vanilla. Or, after 6 months old (and only then), a hint of honey, or of white or brown sugar. But even then, only a sprinkle...in order to develop in baby the sensitive palate of a gourmet.

**A dessert's nutritional range should be carefully put together. It is not about developing a queen's palate, but rather one that appreciates simple delicacies** that can be eaten on their own as a snack or at Sunday brunch, or finish a weekday meal with a smile.

**These delicacies can contain valuable protein and carbohydrates that will fill baby's stomach** after a lunch filled with veggies. Cinnamini Cookies, Pancakes with Maple Syrup, Chocolate Chunk Cookies, Crêpes, etc., are easy to make with a flick of the wrist, thanks to the Babycook.

**Or a water-vitamins-fiber combination after** a pasta supper: a Tropical Treat, a Mango Hedgehog and Marmalade, a Watermelon or Cherry Granité, or perhaps a Strawberry-Rhubarb or Raspberry Crumble.

**And of course the famous protein-calcium duo when baby asks for it.** Fromage Blanc with Walnut crumbs... which provides fat to boot!

**Or even better: a beautiful and healthy mixture of both fruit and dairy products, with the Yogurt Shakes à la carte, created by Chef Dad himself.** He adapted the concept of a milk-shake especially for baby, with a range of different cooked fruits (or raw ones when the time comes).

**Don't forget to wipe away your milk mustache!**

# Desserts and Snacks

Grandma says:

*Make sure that the pieces of crumble are very fine, to avoid swallowing down the "wrong tube!"*

Desserts and Snacks

Delicacies

Summer - Fall

**12** months and up

# Strawberry-Rhubarb Crumble

## This recipe's good points:

*Crunchy and soft, pink and green, sweet and sour... this dessert awakens the senses! Its sweetness satisfies gastronomic explorers. But the nutritional balance of this treat also reassures mom and dad.*

Chef Dad's Advice:

*Leave the leaves on a few of the strawberries that you are using in this recipe. The leaves will help preserve the dessert. And make sure that sweet taste of the strawberries dominates the rhubarb's acidity.*



*Remove the butter from the refrigerator before starting to cook so that it is soft. You can substitute 5.75 oz of wild strawberries or 5.75 oz of raspberries for the regular strawberries in this recipe.*

[ **1h 20** min

**Useful Utensils**

3 small mixing bowls
Plastic wrap
Bowl
Paring knife
Tablespoon
Parchment paper
Baking sheet
Small, clear bowl

**Grocery list for a 1 year old child**

**[ at the market**
5.75 oz ripe strawberries
5.25 oz rhubarb

**[ at the grocery store**
1 cup brown sugar
1/2 cup almond powder
3.5 Tbsp butter
1/3 cup sifted flour

## Here we go!

[ **First, prepare the dough.** Place the butter, almond powder, flour, and 1/4 cup of the sugar in the blending bowl. Pulse twice to obtain a moist, gritty dough. Transfer the dough to a mixing bowl, cover with plastic wrap, and let it rest for about an hour in the refrigerator. During that time, wash the blending bowl, preheat the oven to 350 °F (gas 5) and...

[ **prepare the fruit.** Wash the strawberries under running water, stem them, and place them in the steamer basket. Sprinkle them with some of the sugar (1/3 cup). Cook for 10 minutes (water level 2). Pour a very small amount of the cooking juices into the blending bowl along with the cooked strawberries. Pulse once to obtain a marmalade-like mixture (make sure it's not soupy!). Pour the mixture into a mixing bowl and allow it to cool for about 15 minutes in the refrigerator. Wash the rhubarb stalks under running water and peel them (make sure to remove the stringy fibers). Cut the stalks into small pieces and place them in the steamer basket with the remaining sugar (2/3 cup). Cook for 15 minutes (water level 3). Transfer the rhubarb to the blending bowl, along with 1 tablespoon of the cooking juices. Pulse once to obtain a marmalade-like mixture. Pour it into a mixing bowl and allow it to cool for about 15 minutes in the refrigerator.

[ **To finish it off (once the dough has rested)** lower the oven temperature to 300 °F (gas 3). Line the baking sheet with a sheet of parchment paper. Remove the dough from the refrigerator and crumble it onto the baking sheet. Place in the oven and bake for 20 minutes. Remove from the oven and allow to cool. Spoon a layer of strawberry jam (2 tablespoons) and a layer of rhubarb jam (2 tablespoons) into a small, clear bowl. Then sprinkle with the crumble.

[ Looks good enough to eat!

Mom spreads blueberry or blackberry jam, quince jelly, or chestnut cream onto crêpes for the youngest connoisseurs.

Desserts and Snacks
Delicacies

12 months and up

# Candlemas Crêpes

Winter

[ 5 min, plus cooking time

**Useful Utensils**
Nonstick pan
Small ladle
Paper towel
1 soup bowl
1 dinner plate
Dish towel

**Grocery list for a 1 year old child**

**[ at the cheese shop** 1 "farm-fresh" free-range egg

**[ at the grocery store** 3.5 tablespoons flour
1 tablespoon butter
1/3 cup prepared milk-based pediatric nutritional supplement
...and for the frying pan: grapeseed oil



## Here we go!

[ **First, prepare the batter.** Place the flour, milk, and butter in the blending bowl. Break the egg into it. Pulse 3 times and thin the batter with 1 tablespoon of slightly mineralized water, if necessary. There is no need to let it rest.

[ **Next, the cooking step.** Heat the nonstick pan. Pour a small amount of oil into a soup bowl and soak some of it up with paper towel. Use this to grease the hot pan. Pour a small ladleful of batter into the pan. Immediately roll the pan around from left to right to spread out the batter. Brown the batter for 1 minute. Turn the crepe over (flipping it in the air when you get into the swing of things, to astound your young audience) and brown the other side. Slide it onto a plate and cover it with a clean dish towel so that it does not dry out.

[ Repeat these instructions for each crêpe.

# ...and Crêpes à l'orange

Once your crêpes are ready, melt 1/4 cup of butter in a saucepan over low heat. When the butter starts to color, add a teaspoon of sugar, and let the mixture caramelize slowly. Then add the juice of 1 orange to deglaze. Pour the orange mixture into a baking dish, soak the crêpes in it, and fold them so that they soak up the orange mixture.



### This recipe's good points:

*This recipe is a hit with kids from 1 to 100. The cook loves it because it is extremely easy to make and he or she almost always has the necessary ingredients on hand. Guests love it because it is good enough to ask for seconds. And why not, because it contains protein and complex sugars, which provides the body with what it needs for long-lasting energy or a good night's sleep.*

*Because you don't have to let the batter rest with Babycook, these delicious treats can be added to the menu at the last minute... as long as the butter isn't too cold, making it too hard.*

Chef Dad's Advice:
*Think about adding a pinch of salt to the egg white to help it form stiff peaks. And instead of maple syrup, you can sprinkle the pancakes with powdered sugar.*

Desserts and Snacks
Delicacies

12 months and up

# Pancakes with Maple Syrup

All seasons

[ 15 min (+ 1 h)

**Useful Utensils**
Mixing bowl
Whisk
2 bowls
Soup bowl
Paper towel
Small nonstick blini pan with a removable handle
Small ladle
Wooden spatula

**Grocery list for a 1 year old child**

**[ at the cheese shop** 1 "farm-fresh" free-range egg

**[ at the grocery store** 2.5 Tbsp sugar
1-1/4 cups sifted flour
2 Tbsp yeast
4 Tbsp prepared milk-based pediatric nutritional supplement
1 teaspoon grapeseed oil
1 teaspoon Canadian maple syrup
...or powdered sugar

## Here we go!

[ **To prepare the batter,** start by separating the egg white from the yolk. Place the flour, sugar, and yeast in the blending bowl. Pulse once. Add the egg yolk. Pulse once more. Add the milk and blend with 2 more pulses. Transfer the batter to a mixing bowl and let it rest for at least an hour at room temperature. Preheat the oven to 350 °F (gas 5). Beat the egg white until stiff and gently incorporate it into the batter after it has rested.

[ **Time to cook!** Heat the blini pan. Pour a small amount of oil into a soup bowl and soak some of it up with a paper towel. Use this to grease the hot pan. Turn off the heat. Pour a small ladleful of batter into the pan and... place the pan in the oven. The dough will turn brown and rise. When it rises as high as the sides of the pan, turn the pancake over with a spatula. When both sides are brown (around 3 minutes), remove the pancake and slide it onto baby's plate.

[ Pour the maple syrup over the warm pancake that is crunchy on the outside and soft on the inside. Watch your little guy like his lips!



*Alphonse likes to watch the maple syrup dribble over the hot pancakes in little rivulets.*

**This recipe's good points:**

*A classic British brunch dish... but with Chef Dad's special twist, which makes them even better than the pancakes that Alphonse tasted at his cousins' house in London.*

*Carbohydrates in the flour, B vitamins in the yeast, a team of protein-iron-essential fatty acids in the milk, and the complete nutrition of the egg: a good start to an active day!*

*Sweet, golden maple syrup with its "taste of the Great White North" is a substitute for honey in Canada and has the same qualities (simple carbohydrates and vitamins). Helps kids grow up strong as a lumberjack!*

Chef Dad's Advice:

Serve the cookies with a yogurt shake. They go together so well. You can also substitute white chocolate for the dark chocolate… or use both!

Desserts and Snacks
Delicacies
Winter and All seasons

18 months and up

# Chocolate Chunk Cookies

[ **30** min

**Useful Utensils**

Cutting board
Paring knife
Bowl
Tablespoon
Baking sheet
Silicon baking mat
…or parchment paper

**Grocery list for an 18 month old child**

[ **at the market** 3/4 cup (2.5 oz) pecans

[ **at the grocery store** 1 cup sifted flour
2/3 cup brown sugar
5 oz dark or white chocolate
6 Tbsp butter
1 teaspoon salt

**This recipe's good points:**

*A recipe for those days when you are all bundled up!*

## Here we go!

[ Preheat the oven to 250 °F (gas 2). Line a baking sheet with a silicone baking mat or a piece of parchment paper.

[ Place the walnuts in the blending bowl. Pulse twice. Transfer the "crumbs" to a bowl. Cut the chocolate into big pieces with a knife. Place the butter and sugar into the blending bowl and pulse once. Add the flour and salt and pulse once more. Add the walnuts and the chocolate chunks. Pulse twice.

[ Use a soup spoon to shape the dough into little 1.5 inch long rolls on a cutting board. Cut the rolls into half inch slices. Place the slices on the silicon baking mat or parchment paper on the baking sheet. Increase the oven temperature to 400 °F (gas 6). Bake for approximately 20 minutes.

[ **Serve warm and enjoy right away. Yum!**

**Chef Dad's Advice:**
*In Sweden, these dry cookies are served with a glass of "Fläder Saft," a mixture of cold water with elderberry and blueberry syrup, which is both sweet and bitter. So serve the flavored syrup or juice that your little connoisseur likes the most.*



12 months and up

# Cinnamini Cookies (Pepparkakor)

[ **20** min (+ **3** hours resting time)

**Useful Utensils**

Mixing bowl
Plastic wrap
Silicon baking mat or parchment paper
Baking sheet
Daisy-shaped cookie cutter
Pastry board

**Grocery list for a 1 year old child**

**[ at the grocery store**
1 Tbsp cinnamon powder
1/2 teaspoon clove powder
1/2 teaspoon ginger powder
1 Tbsp sifted flour
2 Tbsp sugar
1/2 cup butter

**[ at the cheese shop**
2 "farm-fresh" free-range eggs
1/2 Tbsp thick crème fraîche

**This recipe's good points:**

*Round and daisy-shaped, thin, and light: these Pepparkakor (pronounced "pepa-coca") are the favorite cookies of Swedish "kids" both young and old! Mi, Alphonse's mom, says that they have «the taste of Scandinavian heather». They are full of good qualities, as well: cinnamon calms the digestive tract; ginger aids digestion; and cloves makes toothaches go away and stimulate the appetite...among other things!*

## Here we go!

[ Take the butter out of the refrigerator beforehand so that it is soft.

[ **Prepare the dough.** Place the flour, sugar, and butter in the blending bowl. Pulse twice. Add the crème, spices, and eggs and pulse twice more. Transfer the dough to a mixing bowl and cover it with plastic wrap. Let the dough rest for about 3 hours in the refrigerator.

[ Preheat the oven to 400 °F (gas 6). Place the silicon baking mat or parchment paper on a baking sheet.

[ When the dough is done resting, roll it out so on a pastry board to a thickness of 1/8 to 1/4 inch. Cut out the dough with the cookie cutter and place the cookies directly onto the silicon baking mat (or parchment paper). Reduce the oven temperature to 350 °F (gas 5). Place the baking sheet in the oven and bake for 15 minutes.

[ **Let cool before tasting... and see them smile!**

Chef Dad's Advice:

*You may vary these recipes to baby's liking, with blackberries, plums, mirabelles, peaches, apricots, or passion fruit. The amount of sugar to be added depends on how ripe the fruit is... and on baby's tastes.*





6 months and up

# Yogurt Shakes à la carte

All seasons

[ 5 min

**Useful Utensils**

Small knife
Cutting board
Tablespoon
Teaspoon
Shatterproof glass

**[ basic ingredients**

1 "just for baby" yogurt, for children 6-12 months old or 1 yogurt made with whole milk for children over 1 ...and 1 tablespoon crushed ice

## Strawberry-Banana Yogurt Shake

**This recipe's good points:**

*A good team! The consistency is a winner: babies love bananas. The nutritional values are rich: the starch and potassium found in bananas compliment the vitamin C in strawberries. But make sure to test baby for a strawberry allergy beforehand.*

**Grocery list for a 1 year old child**

1/2 large ripe banana
1 dozen strawberries
...and about 1 teaspoon sugar

### Here we go!

Wash the strawberries, stem them, and cut them in half. Peel the banana and cut it into slices. Place the fruit in the blending bowl. Blend slightly (1 short pulse). Add the yogurt, crushed ice, and sugar. Pulse once more. Pour into a glass and serve.

## Strawberry-Kiwi Yogurt Shake

**This recipe's good points:**

*Loaded with vitamins and vitality, and dominated by vitamin C.*

*And of course, test for a strawberry allergy before allowing baby to enjoy.*

**Grocery list for a 1 year old child**

1 small ripe kiwi
1 dozen strawberries
...and about 1 tsp sugar

### Here we go!

Wash the strawberries, stem them, and cut them in half. Wash and peel the kiwi, and cut in slices. Place the fruit in the blending bowl. Blend slightly (1 short pulse). Add the yogurt, crushed ice, and a little sugar. Pulse once more. Taste and add a bit more sugar, if necessary. Pour into a glass and serve.

## Raspberry Yogurt Shake

### Grocery list for a 1 year old child

0.33 oz ripe raspberries (6 berries)
...and about 1 teaspoon sugar

### This recipe's good points:

*A pretty pink color, and a good dose of vitamin C.*

### Here we go!

Carefully wash the raspberries and place them in the blending bowl. Blend slightly (1 short pulse). Add the yogurt, crushed ice, and a little sugar (very little if the raspberries are very ripe). Pulse once more. Taste and add a bit more sugar, if necessary. Pour into a glass and serve.

## Blackcurrant Yogurt Shake

### Grocery list for a 1 year old child

2 Tbsp blackcurrants
...and about 1 teaspoon sugar

### This recipe's good points:

*It is said that blackcurrants keep their vitamin C no matter how they are prepared, which is very important in cold winter months!*

### Here we go!

Wash the blackcurrants and place them in the blending bowl. Blend slightly (1 pulse). Add the yogurt, crushed ice, and a bit of sugar. Pulse once more. Taste and add a bit more sugar, if necessary. Pour into a glass and serve.

## Fig-Honey Yogurt Shake

### Grocery list for a 3 year old child

1 nice-looking, ripe fig
...and 1 Tbsp white honey

### Here we go!

Wash the fig, peel it, and cut it into small pieces. Place them in the blending bowl. Pulse once. Add the yogurt, crushed ice, and honey. Pulse once more. Pour into a glass and serve.

### This recipe's good points:

*A good fall recipe that is extremely nourishing and should be reserved for young athletes 3 and up. Figs are rich in sugar (and valued for their fiber), and so is honey.*

# Cooking Clues

## The Babycook Book definition of dishes...

### ...that can be drunk from a bottle, or eaten with a spoon:

- **Bouillon** (Broccoli): cooking juices
- **Gazpacho** (made with tomato and cucumber): cold soup made from summertime vegetables
- **Milk** (made with red or green lettuce): bouillon with a splash of milk
- **Soup**: vegetables that have been cooked and blended, with a more or less liquid consistency
- **Velouté**: smooth soup

### ...that can be eaten with a spoon

- **Brandade**: mix of fish and potatoes
- **Babaganoush**: savory eggplant marmalade
- **Compote**: blended cooked fruit
- **Crumble**: crunchy crust sprinkled over a fruit compote
- **Flan**: dessert made with dairy products and eggs
- **Fondue** (made with tomatoes): savory thin marmalade
- **Gnocchi**: pasta made with cheese
- **Granité**: light syrup, placed in the freezer and scraped into ice shavings with a fork
- **Gratin**: dish placed under the broiler to brown (and cook, if necessary)
- **Marmalade**: slightly blended compote that contains chunks of fruit
- **Mousse**: homogenous and fluffy consistency
- **Stew**: vegetables that have been cooked but not blended
- **Purée:** cooked and blended vegetable(s)
- **Dumpling**: light leavened dough made with fish
- **Tartare**: raw ground fish or meat with seasonings
- **Yogurt-shake**: the yogurt-based version of a milk-shake

### ...that can be eaten with a fork

- **Carpaccio**: thinly cut meat that is marinated and cured by the marinade
- **Meat or Fish Cake:** dish that is soft on the inside and crunchy on the outside

## Cooking Clues:

- **Blanch**: place a food in a saucepan of cold water, cook until the water boils, then remove it
- **Brunoise**: diced vegetables
- **Crush**: cut into irregular sized pieces (= finely chop)
- **Cut**: use a knife to cut into pieces according to a specific technique (julienne or brunoise)
- **English-style**: place food in a saucepan of boiling water and then remove it
- **Julienne**: slice vegetables in the thin strips the size of matchsticks
- **Moisten**: add just enough liquid to cover the food
- **Poach**: cook in a hot liquid
- **Separate**: separate the egg white and yolk
- **Set aside**: place food to the side for use later in the recipe
- **Stem**: remove the stems or stalks (of a fruit or vegetable)
- **Sweat**: cook an ingredient for several seconds without browning, in butter or oil, while stirring
- **Thin**: add a little liquid to a mixture that is too thick
- **Thinly slice**: cut thin slices with a knife

# Chef Dad's Useful Utensils

• Soup bowl • Dinner plate • Large bowl or tub • Bowl (or cup) • Saucepans (small and medium-sized)
• Chinois • Scissors • Small, clear bowl • Wooden spoon • Teaspoon • Tablespoon • Melon baller
• Cherry pitter • Vegetable peeler • Slotted spoon • Daisy-shaped cookie cutter
• Silicon baking molds and mat • Kitchen twine • Whisk • Fork • Mandoline • Paper towel • Plastic wrap
• Parchment paper • Strainer • Paring knife • Pastry brush • Toothpicks • Cutting board • Pastry board
• Baking sheet • Gratin dish (or baking dish) • Small ladle • Nonstick pan • Blini pan
• Plastic containers for preserving food in freezer • Ramekin • Cheese grater
• Mixing bowls (small and medium-sized) • Fabric (small piece of cheesecloth, linen or burlap) • Glass

Also: • Steamer basket…• Plastic spatula…• …and a Baby Cook blender!

As well as a tablecloth, dish towels, and latex gloves for the cook

**Baby's Place Setting**

• Soup bowl (and its saucer) • Dinner plate • Dessert plate and/or small dish
• Sippy cup and lid • Plastic cup • Egg cup
• Ergonomic spoon and fork that don't conduct heat and have no taste
• …and a bottle, until baby doesn't want it anymore!

• Bib with front pocket and/or long sleeves • High-chair or booster seat

# The Age of Reason and...

**Meal Recipes**



**Dessert and Snack Recipes**

# For More Information

**Books...**

• *The Baby Cookbook, Morrow Cookbooks* •
• *Organic Baby & Toddler Cookbook,* DK Adult •
• *The Baby Bistro,* Rodale Books •
• *First Meals,* DK Adult •
• *Larousse Gastronomique,* Larousse •
• *Alain Ducasse's Culinary Encyclopedia* collection, Alain Ducasse •

**www.beaba.com**

**Thank you to:**

Thank you to Jean-Louis Berchet, Christophe Bougouin, and Marie Claveau at Béaba for allowing us to create this book full of Chef Dad's recipes for Babycook moms.

Thank you to David Rathgeber who had the idea to create a book for Alphonse and who adapted his professional recipes for "little connoisseurs."

Thank you to Andrea and Millan, Gaspard and Louise, Léa and Sacha, Lili, Lilou, and, of course, to Alphonse, for tasting the little dishes created especially for them. Thanks to their moms, dads, grandmas, etc., for opening up their kitchens and welcoming the photographer, Jean-Bertrand, who managed to be as discreet as possible!

Thank you to Clémence for enthusiastically collecting all of the necessary elements and for going to the market so we could test the recipes. Thank you to Laurence for so effectively collecting Chef Dad's recipes and making them accessible, and for giving a few good tips to young parents to encourage their baby's growth and awaken his or her taste buds.

And thank you to Anne for her graphic creations and innovations.

**Series Directors**
Héléne Picaud and Emmanuel Jirou-Najou

**Editorial Office**
Marie-Alice Chicou

**Photography**
Jean-Bertrand Augendre

**Graphic Creation and DTP**
Anne Chaponnay

**Translation**
Textra (Hattie Hill - Evelyne Strechinsky)

ISBN: 2-84123-109-7

First published in France in 2004 by Les Editions Culinaires

Printed in France by Aubin Imprimeur

Legal Deposit: November 2004

SPANISH EDITION